Liturgy with Style and Grace

"Reflections": Georgene Wilson, OSF, and Father Ronald Lewinski

Cover art: Mary Jo Huck

Book design: David Sims

Second edition copyright © 1984, Archdiocese of Chicago.
Liturgy Training Publications
1800 North Hermitage Avenue
Chicago IL 60622-1101
1-800-933-1800

FAX 1-800-933-7094

Printed in the United States of America.

ISBN 0-930467-28-0

Liturgy
with Style and Grace
Revised Edition

Gabe Huck

Liturgy Training Publications

This Book and How to Use It

The first edition of *Liturgy with Style and Grace* was published in 1978. Since then the book has gone through several printings, but this represents the first revision of the text. Much of the text has been rewritten, the reflections have been simplified, the bibliography has been updated, and the format has been altered to make the book more readable.

What has not changed is the purpose and structure of the book. This is a book for members of parish liturgy committees and planning teams, for those who have a ministry at the liturgy, for anyone who wishes to learn more about the liturgy. It is for newcomers and for those who need a refresher course. It can be used by one person or a group and can be taken at just about any pace that seems right.

The approach on these pages is to liturgy as something that *people do*. To that extent, it is not an approach from theology, or from history, or from church legislation. All of these are important, crucial, to a full understanding of liturgy. But before we can do our theology, before we can make sense of our history, before we can work with the church legislation, we have to know what it is we are talking about: we have to know liturgy as a certain form of human activity. When we keep a season like Advent, when we have a wedding, when we sing the great Amen or come forward to take communion, when we simply make the sign of the cross: in all these we are doing something that belongs to a human way of expression for the individual and the community. It is a ritual. Only when ministers and planners have some feeling for how we use ritual—as human beings and as Christians—will they know how to approach their work.

What is presented here is an overview. It is to introduce you to liturgy so that you can do it better. The quality of our common prayer of liturgy suffers very often not because we lack a theology or a spirituality, but because we do not do the human things very well. We leave liturgy off by itself somewhere, a domain we visit but are never at home in. Perhaps this book is simply to make us more at home.

You will not find whole programs or detailed approaches in this book. Instead there is a context in which to view the practical problems. A group using this book may find common understandings, a common vocabulary: tools for their work in liturgy. Too often those working with liturgy are overwhelmed with details and have no vision of the whole. The approach here will allow planners and ministers to share a sense for the total way liturgy expresses the life of a parish.

The units have been grouped in six sections.

- First Things. Some basic thoughts are presented here on liturgy and Christian life.

- The Elements of Liturgy. We pray together with words, sounds, gestures, places and objects, and in the way all of these come together.

- Who Does the Liturgy? Here are units on the assembly and the various ministries: presider, lectors, ushers, acolytes and more.

- The Mass. This is here considered in detail.

- Days and Seasons. Prayer has its rhythms through days and years: this is an introduction to the seasons.

- Other Rites. Here are considerations of the liturgies that mark initiation, marriage, sickness and other occasions.

Each of these sections concludes with a short list of resources. Only basic documents and books have been included here.

Within each section are a number of short essays, most of them followed by one or more reflections. These reflections do not always review the essay. More often, they invite the readers to explore some one point in detail.

When this book is used by a group, the leaders will want to draw from each unit additional questions for reflection and discussion. They should allow ample time for those present to bring up the points in each unit that need elaboration or discussion. Participants should be encouraged to read each week's material with pencil in hand to underline, question and make marginal notes. The "Reflections," then, are models suggesting ways to approach the discussion, sometimes through stories, sometimes through critique of current parish practice, sometimes through an expansion of one idea from the unit.

Whether you are reading this book alone or studying it with others, allow it to provoke your own thinking, to stimulate discussion, to send you further in search of our liturgy.

Contents

First Things

What We Mean and Believe

The best of Jewish and Christian tradition tells those concerned with the way prayer happens to beware. Beware of forgetting that the prayers we make together are not religion. Beware of the tricky way appearances and realities have of getting mixed up. Beware of thinking prayer is about rules or methods or special gifts or training.

This line of thought runs through the scriptures. Isaiah put it strongly when he has the Lord speak: "From now on, when you pray with your hands stretched out to heaven, I won't listen. Even though you make many prayers, I will not hear, for your hands are those of murderers; they are covered with the blood of innocent victims." (Is 1:15)

That's one side of the problem for anyone working with the liturgy: it can become its own little world. We know, for example, that beautiful expression in music is a normal element of liturgy. Yet it is not beauty alone that makes liturgy. Likewise, liturgy can be emptied of prayer, of its own very self, when it becomes solely a matter of laws to be fulfilled. Yet, being who we are, we need the laws too: the forms, the traditions that are handed on.

Those scriptures of ours and the deeds of our saints tell us that what is most delicate about liturgy goes beyond beauty and beyond law. People who do the liturgy well, with strength, are people who live lives that need these rituals. We can make the choices and do the things that set up a perfectly fine, well adjusted, perhaps prosperous life that just doesn't need prayer at all. Then we can put our times of liturgy aside or turn them into an art exhibit or a system for keeping God happy.

The other choice is to fashion a life that needs prayer and that needs ritual. The prayer is both the private conversation with the Lord and the repeated patterns which our tradition gives us. The ritual embraces these patterns of praying and includes also the structured ways of keeping feasts and seasons, of fasting and of proclaiming scripture, of professing faith and renouncing evil.

Ritual and prayer are not meant to be present in our lives as obligation, as diversion, as education or as entertainment. They are not there as a nearly magic way to salvation. Rather, they are there because we need them, because without them we could not be ourselves, could not be the church. The liturgy is the various rituals of the assembled church. It is the deed of the assembled church. It is what we who are baptized need to do: the songs we need to sing, the words we need to hear, the gestures we need to make. "Need" because without them we cannot give our lives their gospel shape. In liturgy, we are what we mean to be. The immersion in baptism's waters is the death we die to evil all our lives, is new life we have in Christ. Bread broken and the cup poured out at the eucharist are the sacrifice and sharing we are to be for the world.

The experience of our people has been that a life of faithfulness to the Lord, the constant loving of God and neighbor and self, calls out for ritual expression, is sustained by ritual. *We* are sustained—if the ritual is our deed, if in its beauty and simplicity it can carry and form us.

Quite simply, ritual and life are not strangers in our tradition. They create, nourish and sustain each other.

We Express in Symbols

The kind of prayer that parish liturgy planners and ministers are especially concerned with involves numbers of people. It is the ritual of a community, an assembly. This is something different than ten or a hundred people who happen to be each praying privately in the same space at the same time. It is a matter of the ritual this assembly does. Community rituals can happen on all sorts of occasions, from birthday parties to wakes to football games to wars. They are ways for people to express common attitudes and feelings and understandings in a way that transcends mere speaking.

Consider the wedding. Any society evolves ways to express what the union of a man and a woman means. In some cases, the expressions may live longer than the meanings which gave rise to them (do you know what carrying the bride across the threshold meant to the people who first did it?). Generally there will be a whole series of activites—words, songs, actions, objects—which convey beyond any philosophical or legal or religious or sociological language all that this group wants marriage to mean. In themselves, these things are just elements from life—a ring, a kiss, a dance, hands joined together—but in the context of this community they have all kinds of meanings which express beyond any words what marriage is about. These ritual actions can strengthen that meaning for the particular couples and for all who witness them.

Sometimes we are tempted to treat this matter of ritual as a simple kind of shorthand. In Advent, we often hear that in the advent wreath the circle *means* this, the candles *mean* something else. Certainly there is some value in telling the story behind the advent wreath, and that in fact is what is happening. But the ritual can be robbed of its power when we treat it as a way to teach a lesson, or as an equation where each element has its exact value. Ritual is far deeper. When it is done wholeheartedly and well, ritual touches many layers of ourselves at once.

It is barely right, for example, to say that the wedding ring means that the union is to last forever (the circle), or that it is a sign that these two are bound together. It is really not the ring at all that is the symbol used in this ritual: it is the giving of the ring, the putting on of the ring, the wearing of the ring. Who would dare try to exhaust the meaning of that in words? Rituals are never one dimensional, never just an object, just a word. Within a community of persons who share some vision of themselves and of what life is about, rituals have many dimensions, are always actions inseparable from human beings doing the actions. They are always ambiguous, defying us to neatly classify or explain them.

So in the ritual of the advent wreath: it is not what the candles can be said to stand for that makes it ritual, belief embodied in symbol. Rather, it is the doing of this special prayer: the reverent lighting of the candles in the darkness, with some silence that is gently broken with spoken words and with a music that itself has the rhythm and feeling of this light/darkness cycle in our lives.

Symbols carry our meanings and beliefs—but they carry them, they do not stand still with them. Symbols are not things we can put out on the table, take apart and study. They are things that we do, and thus they entwine themselves with our lives. Only then do they become symbols. Only then can they express what we mean and believe and strengthen in us true meaning and heartfelt belief.

The ritual that the church—the people assembled—does is as much ritual as a birthday party or an inauguration. But it differs from these other rituals for what liturgy expresses in symbol is what these people believe and mean to be the very heart of their existence. Those who believe alike and belong to a common church may share many things: structures of church government, a morality, a creed. But none of these can sustain community, can sustain faith. Only their ritual, their expressing in symbolic ways what they mean and believe, can do this.

Symbols That Carry the Tradition

The symbols with which the church expresses its prayer are not many. Nor are they far removed from everyday human life. They are not unique to the Christian churches, but can be found in a variety of forms among many societies. The most universal of these is probably the sharing of a sacred meal, a rite of eating together which conveys and strengthens the unity of those partaking and their unity with their God. Within the Jewish tradition, such a meal took on several forms, each drawing meanings from the history and faith of Israel. Such a rite is the Passover meal: a night when the people in their own homes, sharing with those in need, tell the same story, share the memories of the same sufferings and deliverance, affirm the same hope, partake of the foods which are themselves bound up with the story, liberation and hope.

But among the Jews there also developed a deep sense for the holiness of every meal, for food and table fellowship as constant occasions to praise and thank God. This would normally be the meal of a family or household together, but on occasion it would be more formal when groups who shared common bonds joined together. Among Jews the development of both the special rituals, such as Passover, and the more common blessing of the household's meals has continued. Among Christians, the tradition of Jesus' last supper and of the other occasions when he blessed and broke bread with his followers shaped their Jewish rituals. The early church said that Christians gathered on the first day of the week for the "breaking of bread." And through all the misunderstandings of later ages, the basic ritual continued: blessing bread and wine in the eucharistic (thanksgiving) prayer, breaking the bread, sharing the bread and wine. Attitudes and emphases have varied through the ages, but the tradition continues. Christians express their faith and common life through their gathering at a table to give thanks over the bread and wine and to share the banquet of the Lord.

A common food and a common drink, the thanksgiving-filled sharing of these, the eating and drinking together which is such a deep and common part of being human: these are the rituals that continue to express our lives as Christians. Their roots are in hunger: for food, for each other, for the Lord. They are then not something terribly theoretical, the realm of the cleric or theologian, but something we know about first because they are so simple, so human.

Much the same is true for the other symbols which have carried our faith from generation to generation. The baptismal washing water, the laying on of hands in blessing and healing and commissioning, the anointing with oils, the singing of praise to God morning and evening: these have marked the church, carried the faith through centuries.

Nothing in the liturgical renewal of recent years has been about replacing these symbols, finding contemporary substitutes. Rather there has been a growing realization that it is our fidelity to such basic rites that has, beyond structures and creeds, given identity to the church. The reform of our rites and their eventual renewal, letting them again be expressions of the living faith of people, is basically an effort to free the symbols from all those things that keep them from doing their work: to free them from magic and superstition, from ministers who are selected without reference to the gifts needed for specific ministries, from dull and mechanical performance, from a spectator mentality. The renewal is about the people, us, possessing the fullness of Christian prayer. This eventually, means a church where the communion meal, the baptism washing, the laying on of hands in healing and forgiveness, are the deepest expressions of who we have been, who we are now, and who we hope to become.

Those who would work for good liturgy can sometimes think that it is an enterprise of interpreting: educating people so that they can translate the symbols into theological language. Not so. Good liturgy occurs when no explanations are needed, when the symbol and the story which surrounds it are done fully, faithfully, powerfully. This will happen when our rites, which are so rooted in all that it means to be human, and which tell all that it means to be Christian, are truly ours to do.

Symbols That Carry the Community

Frequently liturgy planners speak of how difficult good liturgy is in very large parishes: the numbers, the impersonal nature they seem to impose. Even in smaller churches people may have little in common, may feel no need to be anything like a community in order to pray together. We can, sometimes, wonder if consistently good liturgy is compatible with the circumstances today. Many seem content with the mediocre, others just don't want any more of the "changes." Those who have had the opportunity to experience liturgy done well, with reverence and with care and with real celebration, may want very much for this to become the norm for themselves and for everyone—but where to begin?

Begin by accepting the notion that renewing the church's ritual will be a very long task. It has to be, for it cannot happen by decree or by reforming the liturgical books. Nor can it happen by itself, apart from all the efforts and movements that draw people close to the gospel and make for identification and belonging in a church and in a particular church community. Anyway, it just wouldn't be liturgy if it could be renewed apart from all the messy problems of people, of church. They, we, are what liturgy is all about.

But liturgy is an action of a community: people who share at least something of a history, a belonging to one another, a common suffering, a common hope. Liturgy, in fact, helps to create that community because it can be a deep affirmation of what we share, what binds us together. What seems to be clear, though, is that it is very difficult for this to happen until we become far more at home with our ritual. The skills that go into doing the Sunday parish eucharist well—skills needed by every member of the assembly—these are not readily learned when they are used only in the large gathering at the church. These things—how to sing in praise of God, how to be silent and reflect, how to listen to scripture, how to do our great prayer of thanksgiving—are best learned in smaller groups.

The prayer of the larger community somehow depends on the prayer of the little communities, of couples and of families and of individuals. In fact, the strengthening of such praying must never be far from the concern of those who work in liturgy. Many forms of individual and family prayer have rapidly disappeared and little has come to replace them. Our society does not encourage the attitudes and the time that prayer needs. But there is also little in contemporary society that satisfies the hunger for prayer once it is felt.

We need this "back and forth" between the small group and the community. How are we to know what it is we do at the eucharistic prayer and at holy communion unless we experience in the day-by-day course of our lives the giving of praise and thanks to God for our food and for fellowship? This is a matter not only of prayer at table, but of the table itself: of the care we take in this matter of sharing, the thanks we give for food and each other, the way we attend one another's needs, the reverence for the fruit of the earth and work of human hands. How are we to know the psalms as processional and reflective chants in the Sunday liturgy if these psalms, a few of them at least, are not a staple in the prayer of adult and child alike? Can song ever be integral to Sunday liturgy if it is not so to prayer at home?

At home, whether it is one person alone or many, the skills of our ritual are learned: the stuff that makes our liturgy. Those symbols, like thanksgiving and eating, are linked to life in my body, my spirit, my day-by-day movement from birth to death. Here, in the heart of a person, in people at home, are the rhythms of prayer and rite that will need times of coming together with the larger church.

Resources for *First Things*

Bouyer, Louis. *Rite and Man: Natural Sacredness and Christian Liturgy.* Notre Dame: University of Notre Dame Press, 1963.

Classic study of the sacredness of our fundamental rituals.

Kavanagh, Aidan. *Elements of Rite.* New York: Pueblo Publishing Company, 1982.

Some rules, laws, principles and common errors: an honest and often devastating look at Christians and their rituals.

Klauser, Theodor. *A Short History of the Western Liturgy.* New York: Oxford, 1979.

A readable survey of the development of the Christian eucharistic liturgy.

Shaughnessy, James, ed. *The Roots of Ritual.* Grand Rapids: Eerdmans Publishing Company, 1973.

Collection of essays viewing ritual from various disciplines as a human language rooted in our social nature.

The Elements
of Liturgy

To take apart good liturgy and see what makes it run will always give an incomplete answer. The whole is greater than the sum of these parts. Yet if we want to know about liturgy, want to know how to do it well, then we have to look at the elements. We consider four of these here: word, movement, music and environment. They flow through all our church ritual and most of our other rites as well. They are also the stuff of folk art and fine art. They are basic to human expression. In prayer, these elements do their work only when we respect their limits and possibilities, and when we give them all our skill and effort. This section concludes with three units that consider how the elements in liturgy come together to form our prayer.

Word: 1

The Ways We Use Words in Liturgy

Sometimes the efforts at renewal of the liturgy since Vatican II seem to have reduced the liturgy to words. Many places still neglect the times when silence is called for, and so there is constant speaking from beginning to end. Sometimes the words of the prayers and scriptures are increased not only with a lengthy homily but with long and frequent explanations and reminders of the "theme" of the liturgy. Yet we know that when it was well done, the Latin liturgy before the reform was perfectly capable not only of being impressive but of being prayerful—in spite of the fact that not a single word may have been intelligible to the assembly. We should know that liturgy does not work by words alone. More than this, we should now know that when we act as if it does, as if the liturgy *were* words, then what we damage most is the words themselves.

Words in liturgy are not like words on the evening news, or words in the lecture hall, or words in the store or office. What are they like? There are ways we use words for other little rituals in life that show something of how words are used in liturgy.

Consider the greetings and the acclamations. We have rituals to get us through moments of greeting one another. "How are you?" "Good to see you again!" "What's happening?" Or simply: "Good morning!" We also have our ritual words for parting. Such words are often accompanied by a gesture: a wave, a handshake, a kiss. It is not really the content of such words that matters: they are formulas. Does that mean they are insincere? Not at all! Is it insincere to play a role? Is Richard Burton insincere when he becomes King Lear? Obviously, a person can give an insincere greeting, can hold back, can be miles away from the person instead of present to that person. The words can be the same. They are formulas we have, formulas that come and go with generations, for easing the first and last moments we have together. Just so with these words in liturgy. They are formulas, and can be left empty and insincere, or filled with our presence. They usually belong to the presider and to the assembly. "The grace and peace . . ." "Amen." "The Lord be with you." "And also with you." "Go in peace." "Thanks be to God." We do play a role when we say these, but that is what gives them their potential.

Another ritual use of words: acclamations. Acclamations are, by their nature, for everybody. They are the "Hooray!" and the "Viva!" of the liturgy. They are the ritual words like "Alleluia," "Amen," and "Holy, holy" that belong to everybody. In the flow of the ritual they have to be done with great strength and so should nearly always be sung. More on this in the units on music.

And there are other ways we use words in liturgy. There are the prayers that are led by the presider. At Mass, these are the opening prayer, the prayer over the gifts, the eucharistic prayer, the prayer after communion. These are nearly always addressed to the Father and often need moments of silence to prepare for them. They are spoken by one in the name of all present. They are words of the church that are rooted in the words of the scriptures and our tradition. They are formal. With time the English prayers will be chosen for their great beauty, for words that bear the weight of repetition, that open every new meaning to those who hear them.

Litanies are another ritual use of words. Chanting often serves their nature, for litanies build on constant repetition of a refrain. At Mass, the penance rite is often cast in the form of a litany; the prayers of intercession and the "Lamb of God" are also litanies.

Words of invitation are used at liturgy. "Let us pray," "Let us give thanks," and the invitations to join in prayers of intercession, to exchange the peace greeting and to join in communion are all words of this kind. The invitation helps to center attention, call us together, point toward what we are about to do.

Words in liturgy have all sorts of uses. In fashioning a steady and strong liturgy for the community, it helps to know just how words are being used.

Reflections

Many of the words we use at liturgy are repeated frequently either within the same act of worship or from week to week. Using these words again and again makes us feel at home with them. Familiarity can free us to pray better.

But there is also a danger with ritual words. They can lose their meaning and become empty and lifeless unless we make a conscious effort to put our spirit behind them.

1. What are some common ritual words that tend to become lifeless?
2. How can music help our words?
3. Are there any measures we can take to use our ritual words more carefully?

Word: 2   Scripture and Reflection

Whenever the church gathers, the scriptures are present. At very short prayers, as at meal time, this may be only in the form of a few words that echo some song or prayer of the scriptures. But at eucharist, at reconciliation, at the anointing of the sick, weddings, and morning and evening prayer, funerals, the scripture is present as the fundamental element—that is, the foundation—of the liturgy.

How do we think about scripture, these words from the church's book, in the liturgy? Most simply, as the telling of our story. The search for "roots" in recent years has made us all aware of how there is a story that connects us with our past, tells us much of our most personal history, identifies us among all the peoples of the earth. Any tribe of people that remains closely bound together does so in great part because of the story that they continue to tell to explain to themselves and to their children who they are. Such a story most often will involve a whole view of the world, the relations among creatures, the place of the gods. More sophisticated nations do not lose this need for common story; something of this is seen in national independence days.

We have also the universal phenomenon of fairy tales. Here is a worldwide language in which adults find ways of passing on to the next generation the common story of all humankind: the struggle of good and evil, the suffering of the innocent, the things that happen beyond our control, the coming vindication of the good. Stories talk about such things in a way that touches the mind and heart and spirit.

And that is basically why we continue to read the scriptures. We grow up in to the cycle of stories. The story may be a real narrative as such or it may be a song, a genealogy, a group of laws, an exhortation, a vision, a warning, a parable, a prophecy. Such are the makings of the larger story. On most Sundays, we read more or less in order through one of the gospels, and also through the other apostolic writings, the epistles. During seasons or at holidays—and when a special occasion is kept, some parts of our story that revolve around that day are read. Often the reading from Hebrew Scriptures sounds a note which is echoed in the gospel reading. (This is never to be taken as if the first were merely a preparation and the latter the reality. The church has clearly said that the validity of the Hebrew Scriptures is in no way changed by the existence of the gospels and other apostolic writings. Rather, the gospel "echo"—as when the gospel tells of Jesus curing a deaf man after the Hebrew Scripture has spoken of the reign of God as a time when the deaf will hear—shows how strong is the need for the Christian to know the

Hebrew Scriptures. Jesus and the apostles knew them. If we are to understand their words and lives, we must make their scriptures our own.)

In many tribes, it is the grandparents, the elders, who tell the stories at times of festival or at times of tragedy. They have lived the story most deeply in their own lives; they know that the story in fact tells their lives, tells it better than an autobiography, tells it at a level deeper than dates and places. That, of course, is not necessarily a function of age. We entrust our story to those who can capture and keep the attention of the assembly, those whose lives reflect their love of our scriptures, those who are deeply aware of just how this story and this people belong together.

Yet another use of words in liturgy, one always related to scripture, is the homily. Homilists reflect on our lives and our times in light of the story which we have heard. Words in the homily are not scholarly explanations of scripture, nor pious exhortations, nor rambling personal notes. A homily may be in many styles, but always it tries to let the way some particular scripture has touched the speaker find an echo in the listeners.

Reflections

1. The other day my niece said to me: "Tell me again how my daddy told his first grade teacher that he wanted to go home, and she thought he said he had to go to the bathroom so she said, 'Go,' and he left the school and started walking home. But then he came to the street and remembered he wasn't allowed to cross the street without his sister, so he stood there crying. And that's where you found him and brought him back to school."
Obviously she knew the story! What she wanted was an elder to tell it again.

2. Although we use the scriptures every time we gather for prayer, it takes a long time to make them a part of our lives. If we want the word to really be effective at liturgy, we have to think about making the scriptures more intelligible through nonliturgical channels such as the parish bulletin and adult education.
In addition to the homily, how can a parish community make the scriptures more a part of our lives?

Movement: 1

Our Tradition
of Body and Prayer

Try to have a ritual sometime without moving. At a birthday party, no lighting the candles, no blowing them out, no clapping after "Happy birthday to you!" At the St. Patrick's Day Parade, no marching, no raising the glass. Before the baseball game, no standing or removing hats for the national anthem. Even if you somehow planned such a ritual, something like a Quaker meeting or yoga meditation with everyone sitting very still and silent, then the very "not movingness" has become itself a ritual in which words are not spoken and in which there is no music of any kind. But to do something that is important and that is shared among people without using the body in ritual is unimaginable.

In speaking of the way we use our bodies in our prayer together there is one obvious distinction. Sometimes religious rituals involve great spontaneous movement. Some pentecostal churches have made this especially important, allowing and encouraging individuals to manifest the Spirit in jumping, clapping, dancing. (Many who would not at all welcome this sort of ritual in their churches do not mind it at all when it happens in the frenzy of an important football game.) In some parts of the Catholic church, rituals have evolved which allow such bodily expression. Such, however, are not part of the experience of most Christians of European background.

But all of us experience a more controlled use of the body in our common prayer. Catholics have developed and preserved such gesture as a vital part of our worship. Consider genuflecting, the various ways of making the sign of the cross, kneeling and standing, striking the breast, bowing the head at the name of Jesus, folding the hands, the gesture of taking communion in the hand. These are common to everyone. We also know the gestures which go especially with the ministry of the presider: extending the arms, raising the hands, deep bows, blessing gestures, the many gestures associated with various objects (swinging the censer, kissing the gospel book, raising the bread and cup).

Our gestures now are too often "privatized"; they are also reduced somewhat, often done mechanically and without reverence, without grace.

Common gesture in our worship is a way to let the whole person pray, and a way to manifest that this is the prayer and action of a church, the one body of Christ. Even more, common gesture in worship helps to bring this about. It is not, of course, a matter of just any gesture done in any way. Like words, gestures can be halfhearted and insincere, testimony to our indifference. We seek gestures that show respect for the body, a respect that is deep within a church that believes in the incarnation; without such gestures, the praying is partial.

"The liturgy of the Church has been rich in a tradition of ritual movement and gestures. These actions, subtly, yet really, contribute to an environment which can foster prayer or which can distract from prayer. When the gestures are done in common, they contribute to the unity of the worshiping assembly." (From *Environment and Art in Catholic Worship* by the Bishops' Committee on the Liturgy, 56)

Reflections

1. What body rituals do you go through from the time you awake until the beginning of the first task of the day that bring you in touch with other people?
2. Name a few of your family gestures (think broadly).
3. What gestures are you comfortable with in prayer? Has that changed through the years?

Movement: 2 From Here to There

The way one of the ministers or the whole assembly gets from here to there in the liturgy is a good illustration of what happens within a ritual when something practical has to be done. The presider in the back of the room, having greeted people as they arrive for the liturgy, now needs to be in front to welcome everyone and lead the opening prayer: a procession is needed. The deacon is at the chair and it is time for the gospel: a procession. The people are in their benches and it is time to share communion: another procession.

But processions are sometimes for their own sake: on Palm Sunday, Corpus Christi, the feast of a patron saint. Here there is festivity and display, and the procession itself may be the ritual.

Getting from here to there in a ritual manner, for a practical purpose or to have a good time or to display something important—happens frequently outside religious rituals. Parades are rites where such movement is the main means of expression. In a good parade, it is worth noting, one can never say that the celebrants are limited to the people on the floats and in the bands: rather, the celebrants include these and all others along the way. Everyone is swept into the festivity. Sometimes it may be the display of ethnic pride that occasions the parade, sometimes the ritual movement of the newly inaugurated president from the Capitol to the White House, sometimes the beginning of the Christmas shopping season in the Thanksgiving Day parade, sometimes the memory of an event as in Memorial Day parades, sometimes the importance of a vision for a better society as in a Labor Day parade.

And there are simpler sorts of parades and processions to get those with some special part to play from here to there. The special entrance procession of the players at an athletic contest, for example, or the arrival of movie stars on an opening night, or the entrance of a judge into the courtroom. And some processions seem to happen in similar ways whether or not the ritual is given any religious meanings by its celebrants: the procession of the bride (and perhaps the groom) to the place where the vows will be exchanged, or the procession (motorized or on foot) behind the casket when someone is being buried.

We all have some sense for when processions are effective and when they are not. We all know something of how a procession that is done but once a year can be handled, and how different must be a procession that happens every Sunday. We can name the elements that makes these work. Why is the way certain presiders enter the assembly in itself a powerful statement about who we are and why we are here? Why can others move through the same path and end up in the same place and nothing at all is felt about the who or the why? Or, at the gospel, why can one way of doing the procession itself proclaim that we are to rise and acclaim the good news and another leave people wondering if they are supposed to stand? Why does the taking of the holy communion in some cases look like a bunch of people shuffling up for a private and hasty exchange with the minister, and in other cases look like a community sharing one meal, the body and blood of Christ? As with so many parts of ritual, it is not just a matter of saying: "We will have a procession. So-and-so will go with Father from here to there." It is a matter of timing. A matter of pace. A matter of bearing. A matter of space. A matter of grace. A matter of reverence. A matter of sensing what this procession right here is about: entrance processions are not like gospel processions; communion processions are not like exit processions. Each has its own character. This becomes critical not only at eucharist, but at special celebrations: weddings, funerals, baptisms.

"Processions are for the people who move and who like to be moved, for people who have strong religious convictions and like to show them, for people who—by training, experience or intuition—know how much the body in its simple movement of walking brings to the mind and to the spirit in fostering religious experience. Processions are for people who have a sense for symbolic gestures and a feel that the correlations of feet (which walk) and hands (which carry: palms, flowers, song sheets, rosaries, candles) and voices (which sing and pray), that this harmonizing of three existential signs creates a very strong and supporting pattern of witnessing and praise." (Regina Kuehn in *Liturgy 70*, February 1978)

Reflections

1. Rituals tend to order our lives or disorder them. Consider your rituals in getting from home to church and back home again. Do they order your life? What quality, positive or not, do they add to your life?

2. List the various processions in your community's worship experience. Don't forget wedding processions, funeral processions, processions to the font, processions for ashes or candles or palms. What is it that makes a good procession good? What is it that can make processions lifeless and unappealing? What affect could music, color, choice of participants, banners and route make? Would some processions be better outside the church building?

Movement: 3   # How Does It Work?

Movement can be thought of in three areas that are common to every liturgical celebration: posture (how and when we stand, sit, kneel), processions, gestures. It might then be well to look at the Sunday Mass, since that is the most familiar ritual, and see these at work.

Posture. We do not arbitrarily assign meaning to postures. We try to know from experience something of what a posture feels like, yet we see from various cultures that for one people sitting may show reverence, for another standing expresses this. And we know other things: that going very quickly back and forth from one posture to another accomplishes nothing but distraction; that being *told* to sit, to stand to kneel is hardly worthy of an assembly that celebrates liturgy regularly. There are two things at stake: letting our posture express and strengthen our devotion (why, for example, we usually stand up to cheer), and letting the posture keep a good rhythm during the ritual (why we need a seventh inning stretch).

We sit to relax, we sit to listen or to watch. What moments at Mass make sitting the proper posture? And what is kneeling good for? For sorrow? For adoration? Is there something about kneeling that is good for making a moment more private, more inward? And standing? We rise to greet people, we rise to honor someone, we rise when we are filled with excitement. Now at liturgy on a given Sunday we may not feel like listening at this moment, or like acclaiming at another. But at liturgy all present give themselves to the ritual, enter into the prayer. The postures one takes are those that over the long haul can help the ritual do its work, help prayer to happen in a very real way. How we sit, how we stand, how we kneel—these are crucial to the spirit. This is all the more true for the ministers whose posture may inspire (or drive to distraction) those who can see them. We know that sloppiness is contagious; we hope that care and reverence are also.

Processions. This was discussed in the previous section. We need to have a feeling for what is done uniquely in each procession: the entrance, gospel, preparation of gifts, communion, exit. Who is involved? How are they prepared? Practicing how to carry oneself, learning how to carry a candle or a cross or a plate—these come more naturally to some than others. The presence of auxiliary ministers at communion was primarily to give this rite its plain meaning: one meal. Yet the arrangement of the ministers and the way the procession happens can destroy this. How can each procession help the ritual be good prayer?

And gestures. Those with specific ministries have more gestures than the assembly. How do we move from telling an acolyte what a bow is, to the natural grace that should mark the bow? Or from explaining to the lector how high to hold the book to a sense of honoring our sacred scriptures? Or from noting that the presider is to gesture with his words of greeting, to the full participation of eyes, hands, arms—whole person—in the greeting? We need practice, learning from others, getting the feel for it. Then the larger problem: the assembly, too, should have its gestures and these should be modeled and advocated. Can the sign of the cross be a truly common gesture? Could we also raise our hands in praise or join them in solidarity? Could we bow our heads when we are asked to do so before the blessing?

This is a difficult area. Much in our culture reduces us to spectators, wants us to be embarrassed if a genuflection shows adoration or raised hands show praise. But like it or not, only whole people can enter into ritual.

Reflections

1. Try to move the assembly to a standing posture by slowly and deliberately raising your arms while looking directly at their faces. See if the assembly won't learn to bow more gracefully when all the ministers at the altar, including the young acolytes, prayerfully bend their bodies in a bow. Will the assembly learn to reverence the sign of the cross if all the ministers at the altar make it slowly and boldly?

2. Make a list of all the gestures and postures used by the congregation and ministers. How would you note the appropriateness, the gracefulness and the prayerfulness of these bodily movements?

The Sound of Our Prayer

To begin thinking about music in our liturgy, we have to get rid of the idea that music only means singing hymns, whether ancient or modern, classical or contemporary. Instead, try to think first about this: what is the sound of people at prayer? One can begin working on that by noting the characteristics of the sounds at other human assemblies. What are the sounds of people at a banquet? What are the sounds of people at a horse race? What are the sounds of a PTA meeting? What are the sounds of an auction? What are the sounds of the classroom? What are the sounds of the political convention? What do human voices do, other than communicate information, in these various situations? If you heard tape recordings of each without any identification, could you "name the assembly"?

What we do with our voices is a vital part of the occasion. The association between situations and their sounds becomes very close for us: just imagine watching a movie of a horse race with the sound track from a funeral parlor. But what is the sound of people at liturgy? We are only learning. Patterns up to two decades ago were established when nearly all the active parts in the liturgy were taken by the priest. The people were spectators from whom few sounds were expected. The sounds then were the soft Latin, the bell ringing, the tabernacle door closing, the censer clanging, the cruets hitting against the chalice, the noise of people standing and kneeling. Perhaps there was music from a choir or an organist.

We know also some sounds that do not make for prayer: The "read together" liturgy, priest and people alike following in their little books reading their lines. We also know that trying to sing three or four hymns in the course of the Mass does not change this much; it only gives a feeling that "now we'll stop for song." The sounds we are going to make in prayer should be more integral to the prayer than that; they are, in fact, the way prayer gets into the voice. That is not just a matter of words. It is first a matter of sounds. We do not sing to communicate information or to drill in truths: we sing because there is life and faith and church. We can rejoice, we can be troubled, we can recall, we can hope! We can do so much that shatters the flatness of the times. But that calls for sounds—from our voices and the instruments people have made, from bells and hands clapping and feet walking. It calls for sounds that can be louder and softer, higher and lower, faster and slower than everyday speech.

In their statement on music in the liturgy, the United States bishops said: "Music should assist the assembled believers to express and share the gift of faith that is within them and to nourish and strengthen their interior commitment of faith. It should heighten the texts so that they speak more fully and more effectively. The quality of joy and enthusiasm which music adds to community worship cannot be gained in any other way. It imparts a sense of unity to the congregation and sets the appropriate tone for a particular celebration. . . . Music can also unveil a dimension of meaning and feeling, a communication of ideas and intuitions which words alone cannot yield." (*Music in Catholic Worship*, 23–24)

Our need for this "quality of joy and enthusiasm" makes it vital to have a sense for the sound of our prayer. That does not only mean whether a piece is rendered well, though that is important. It means a sound that creates a mood, expresses and deepens an attitude. Musicians can facilitate this sound through playing the organ and other instruments, through helping the assembly sing, through training large and small choirs who have their own sounds to contribute to the common prayer.

Music surrounds us today. Fine music is more accessible to all of us than at any time in history. The kinds of music that can be heard are many and marvelously varied. More than ever, people have an interest in good music, in playing an instrument. We are not *always* spectators! The sound of people praying will be grand when we know our need for music and seek leaders who know how to release this power.

Reflections

1. Choosing the right music for worship is not just finding words to match the texts of the day. The mood or tonal character of a piece may influence the worship as much if not more than the words. Examples?

2. Sometimes, too, the instrument used for a piece of music may suggest a particular mood that would not be created were any other instrument used. If "For all the saints" were used at the end of a funeral liturgy accompanied by a full brass choir, it would certainly create a different mood than if it were accompanied by a single flute. Examples?

3. Do the people sing the liturgy? Take those three words—people, sing, liturgy—seriously.

Musical and
Pastoral Judgments

The 1972 statement of the Bishops' Committee on the Liturgy entitled *Music in Catholic Worship* is basic to any solid approach to good liturgy. In one section of this document, three criteria are proposed in selecting music for the liturgy: that it be good music, that it be pastorally suitable, and that it do the work that the liturgy calls for. Here we want to consider the first two of these judgments.

The bishops ask: "Is the music technically, aesthetically and expressively good?" The importance given this judgment is backed up: "This judgment is basic and primary and should be made by competent musicians" (26). Because worship is an activity of the whole person, because it is meant to engage us in spirit and in mind, in body and in heart and in soul, the elements of worship are those human arts which do touch us deeply, in every part of our lives. The place of music in such an activity is obvious. More than any other means of human expression, music can convey any human emotion, conviction, humor, remembrance. Music is so universal, so much a part of every life.

Our own tradition has used that collection of songs known as psalms since long before the time of Jesus. To these the early church added new words and melodies to express their own experiences of the Lord. Through centuries and cultures, the music of various peoples allowed the church to sing. In the best moments we had strong music in which all could participate, and other music more suited to those with gifts and training. Local churches supported and encouraged the work of the talented musicians in their midst.

It is to our best tradition that the church is now called. At every level, the musical judgment must be made by competent musicians. The document explains why: "Only artistically sound music will be effective in the long run. To admit the cheap, the trite, the musical cliché often found in popular songs on the ground of instant liturgy is to cheapen the liturgy, to expose it to ridicule and to invite failure. Musicians must search for and create music of quality for worship. . . . They must . . . find new uses for the best of the old music. They must explore the repertory of good music used in other communions. They must find practical means of preserving and using our rich heritage of Latin chants and motets." (26–27) There is another point about the musical judgment: It is important not to confuse style with value. Because worship takes shape through the use of art forms, there is a need to choose over and over again between various styles.

The musicians who can best minister to the praying church are those able to sense what styles will enhance the prayer, will assist the local church in its sound, and will let the words and melodies of the liturgy extend into people's lives. Beyond training in music, then, the musician who is entrusted with this judgment by the local church must be sensitive to tastes and abilities and open to a variety of styles of good music. This, in effect, is what the document calls "the pastoral judgment." "It is the judgment that must be made in this particular situation, in these concrete circumstances. Does music in the celebration enable these people to express their faith, in this place, in this age, in this culture?" (39) Here, of course, the musician must work closely with others who are involved in responsibility for the community's worship and must listen closely to the people, sometimes trying to hear what they really mean beneath what they say.

The musical and pastoral judgments, then, are not only about the quality of the pieces selected. They are also about competency in their use. On the parish level, that often means hard questions about well-intentioned volunteers. But at least the goal is clear: good music, well executed, a strong expression of this parish's faith.

Reflections

1. Good music does not just happen. It takes good musicians and good instruments and a realistic budget to create good music at worship. It is unfair to expect an untrained volunteer to do all we have come to desire of music at liturgy. Either we have to budget for futher training, or we must hire more professional people to undertake the ministry of music. Every parish that is serious about good liturgy must also be serious about its budget. Good instruments, good musicians, and sufficient books and scores are necessary ingredients. What is the parish music budget? How often is it revised?

2. How much variety is there in the music you use? How much steadiness?

3. Who makes the final judgment on the music to be used for liturgy?

Music: 3　　　　　# The Liturgical Judgment

Not all music that is good, not even all music that is good for this congregation, will be good music for this congregation at this moment in this particular liturgy. For the liturgy makes its own demands. *Music in Catholic Worship* sums it up: "The nature of the liturgy itself will help to determine what kind of music is called for, what parts are to be preferred for singing and who is to sing them" (30).

"What kind of music is called for" points to our need to probe specific moments in the liturgy. In a liturgy of the word, whether at the Mass or on other occasions, there is need for a kind of music that is supportive but not demanding, music that allows the images created by the scriptures and fostered by moments of silence to find voice in familiar refrains (the verses sung by the cantor or choir).

At other moments, the liturgy calls for acclamations: "It is of their nature that they be rhythmically strong, melodically appealing, and affirmative" (53). At Mass, the ritual needs such acclamations before the gospel and several times within the eucharistic prayer. They are a form of song for which no book is needed. They are to be known "by heart," by the heart. They have a crucial work to do in the most expressive moments of our prayer. A congregation needs a repertoire of these acclamations. They cannot be recited: it is a contradiction in terms. Singing is the only choice, but the music must be good enough to bear repetition as the acclamations are used many times each year, over the years. Their function in prayer is lost when it is necessary to announce them. The intonation by the cantor or a few notes of instrumental introduction should be sufficient to draw everyone present (all ministers included) into strong singing.

There are moments in liturgy where the music needed is a strong phrase repeated over and over. This is the litany, a prayer that builds through repetition. It is a prayer form that the church has known and used often and well, as in the chanting of the litany of the saints. Today we know it in the prayers of intercession, some forms of the penance rite, and the "Lamb of God."

Litanies are prayers that work through the rhythm of listening and responding and so are not dependent on the participants following along in a book. Eyes and hands (in all these kinds of music considered so far) are best freed from the printed page. Like acclamations and refrains, litanies do not do their work at the intellectual level alone: taking in and reflecting on the meaning of the words being sung. They work at a far deeper level, where the rhythms of the singing create a prayer that embraces the whole person. Music is meant to do that in liturgy.

Yet another common kind of music that suits certain moments within the liturgy is the hymn. For this, a book is usually needed. Hymns are best suited to moments that prepare for and conclude the liturgy: they can carry us into our prayer together and provide grand moments of conclusion for the prayer.

The forest is as important as the trees: how all the music works together, makes the liturgy musical, gives shapes and feel to the entire service. Very different styles of music may often be well used within a liturgy, even contributing to this integrity.

The liturgical judgment, "what kind of music is called for," is also about the seasons, about the way that musicians and liturgy planners must listen, reflect, and try to identify the sound of an Advent or a Lent: the rhythms, various instruments, moods that embody the seasons. With great consistency within each season, and from year to year, the familiar sounds make us at home in the church.

Reflections

1. Some congregations just don't want to sing. They seem to be absolutely bored or else too stubborn to participate. Sometimes they have reason to be bored! All the hymns sound the same. They may never have been taught the hymns or acclamations properly. They may be asked to sing the same hymns too often. Or they never hear the same hymn twice. Sometimes a congregation is too stubborn to sing because the text is printed too small to be read comfortably. Or there's no one to lead them. Or they don't sing because none of the ministers sings. In some places the acoustics are so bad that no one can hear the others singing and so they aren't encouraged by a good supporting sound. At times the organist is so poor that the congregation has never heard the same hymn or acclamation played twice in the same way, and they're just tired of trying to guess which way the rhythm will move.

2. Make a list of your congregation's repertoire. Include hymns, acclamations, psalms, litanies. Then divide the selections by their use at liturgy, and by the seasons of the year. What areas are strong? Where is work needed? Would a year's program for improving, not just increasing, the repertoire be helpful (the problem might be the quality of present selections)?

Environment: 1
People and Places

When we meet to pray, we meet somewhere. Concern for the environment of prayer is that simple. What is that "where"? How can it serve the prayer that is to be done? How do we shape our spaces and how do our spaces shape us?

The beginning point may be as simple as the word "church." Christians in the first centuries would have wondered about expressions like "I'll meet you in front of the church," or "We're going to renovate the church," or "Is this church fireproof?" The building where these early Christians met to pray was called the *domus ecclesiae*, "the house of the church." The church was the assembly, the people, the faithful. Whether their terminology would be better for us is not so important as what it tells us about their thinking: the first consideration was the people. A place for the people to gather could always be found.

This primacy of people has been emphasized by the 1978 statement of the Bishops' Committee on the Liturgy, *Environment and Art in Catholic Worship.* "To speak of environmental and artistic requirements of Catholic worship, we have to begin with ourselves—we who are the Church, the baptized, the initiated." (27) Begin with ourselves: who we are, what we are like, what our needs for prayer are, what we would find to be a true home for ourselves, a house in which we can pray. "Among the symbols with which liturgy deals, none is more important than this assembly of believers." (28)

Nothing about the space where we gather is to dominate us when we are praying. "The most powerful experience of the sacred is found in the action of the assembly: the living words, the living gestures, the living sacrifice, the living meal. This was at the heart of the earliest liturgies. Evidence of this is found in their architectural floor plans which were designed as general gathering spaces, spaces which allowed the whole assembly to be part of the action." (29)

Every consideration about the room (whether new or old) and the objects which are placed in it is to grow from this feeling that liturgy is the work of this assembled people, this church. What will help these people pray? What will care for the very best that each person is capable of and not cater to the culture's low estimate of our human capacity for beauty and for sharing? What will bring us from thinking about people as audience, or as many individuals praying, to "concerns for feelings of conversion, support, joy, repentance, trust, love, memory, movement, gesture, wonder" (35)?

What do we know of rooms that seem to have a deep respect for the people who will occupy them? We can think of various spaces that we know: theaters, stores, schools, offices, libraries, hospitals, prisons, factories, homes. One quality we are looking for could be called hospitality. Obviously, such a quality cannot be separated from hospitable people—yet there is something in the physical environment that may invite or may discourage this, something that makes it easier or harder for us to feel welcome, comfortable, at home. We know this quality when we meet it or miss it in a neighbor's home, or a doctor's office. It is not so simple as the color of the walls or the fabric in the drapes, or the carpet being clean or dirty. These things have something to do with how the space makes us feel, but hospitality is about how they all come together, what they do to us as a whole.

Certainly one part of this experience of hospitality is beauty: a space that is beautiful, objects that are beautiful elevate the human spirit; they do welcome us and welcome our prayer. Another part, which must be kept as a balance, is simplicity: without this, the space may not witness to the gospel which we have accepted, and so the space would never welcome Christian prayer. These two things are often in some tension. Gradually, the notion of a space that is hospitable, that reflects and helps create the spirit of the people who gather there, may help to resolve such tensions or at least hold them in balance.

Finally, the truly hospitable environment "disappears" in the hospitality of the people. Space leads toward, fosters, never stands in the way of people's actions. "As common prayer and ecclesial experience, liturgy flourishes in a climate of hospitality: a situation in which people are comfortable with one another, either knowing or being introduced to one another; a space in which people are seated together, with mobility, in view of one another as well as the focal points of the rite, involved as participants and not as spectators." (11)

Reflections

1. What effect does environment have on your daily attitudes? Compare the environment of different homes, grocery stores, libraries and the like. How can the environment work for or against what is supposed to happen in the place? How do the people there reflect and/or contribute to the environment?

2. The renewal of the liturgy calls for a renewal in the place where we pray—more than just changing the sanctuary furniture. The participation of the assembly, the variety of ministries, and the ritual itself dictate a reshaping of the whole space. Search out places noted for good liturgical space, new or renovated. Discuss the worship area in light of the bishops' statement on environment and art.

Environment: 2

Quality and Appropriateness

Acceptance of our prayer as something for the whole person—body, mind, senses, imagination, emotions, memory—has been the constant, if sometimes unwilling and barely alive, glory of our Catholic prayer. We have maintained that the eating and drinking had to happen, the water had to flow, the scripture had to be told. We have said to put a good cloth on the altar table, light the candles, kiss the cross, burn the incense, lay on the hands. Yet, as *Environment and Art in Catholic Worship* acknowledges, we let the symbols shrivel up, tried to make them more manageable and efficient. Now we look for good criteria for the arts with which we form our prayer. Two such demands that liturgy can make on the arts are named in this document: quality and appropriateness. These can well be applied to music, to the spoken word, to movement. Here, though, we consider them in relation to the environment, and specifically to the objects which we use in our prayer.

"Quality is perceived only by contemplation, by standing back from things and really trying to see them, trying to let them speak to the beholder. . . . Quality means love and care in the making of something, honesty and genuineness with any materials used, and the artist's special gift in producing a harmonious whole, a well-crafted work." (20) What does that mean when taken off the page and into our church buildings? Take a look at that Easter candle by the font. Love and care in the making of it? Is it honest? Genuine? Well crafted? Contemplate that candle. What does it say to you? For that is the point: we have too long been trying to say with words what things can say for themselves. If there is quality, then it evokes contemplation and—lo and behold!—the work of art will speak for itself!

More than that, it will say something about what we mean. That is what can happen with liturgy. The bread and wine, the water of baptism, the laying on of hands in forgiveness: we are not here to tell each other what these things mean. Rather, in the sharing of bread and wine, in the washing with water, in the laying on of hands, we learn what we mean. To stifle the work of these symbols is to stifle our own selves.

And the second criterion is appropriateness. That means that the art "must be capable of bearing the weight of mystery, awe, reverence, and wonder which the liturgical action expresses" (21). Is it clear why good liturgy contents itself with the honest things, as beautiful and simple as they can be? "Bearing the weight" is exactly right. The plastic "candle," the water that can't get out of the clogged aspergillum, the banner that carries only a slogan, the wafers that give no sign of being real bread—

these break under the weight of mystery, of wonder. What can bear that weight except honest things, things that are what they appear to be, and so awaken awe and reverence for what is? The building, the book of scriptures, such are "appropriate" when they can bear the weight of mystery "so that we see and experience both the work of art and something beyond it" (22).

Something is appropriate when it serves the liturgy. Is the shape of the room at the service of the assembly's prayer? Is the lighting such that it will enhance the prayer? Is the room hospitable, welcoming, human, warm? Does the vessel that holds the bread serve the liturgy by making that bread visible? Learning what question to ask will be half the task.

Again, as with music, the churches need to support those who have the gifts and the training to bring quality and appropriateness to every object used in the liturgy. The bishops' statement notes: "A major and continuing educational effort is required among believers in order to restore respect for competence and expertise in all the arts and a desire for their best use in public worship. This means winning back to the service of the Church professional people whose places have long since been taken by 'commercial' producers, or volunteers who do not have the appropriate qualifications. Both sensitivity to the arts and willingness to budget resources for these are the conditions of progress so that quality and appropriateness can be real." (26)

Reflections

1. What is your favorite room? What elements make it such: beauty, size, shape, color, other things? And is it only this, or is it also the people you have shared it with who bring quality to it?
2. Is the shape of the room at the service of the assembly's prayer? Is the room hospitable, welcoming, human, warm?

Some Specifics

Some aspects of the worship space require special attention. All quotes are from *Environment and Art in Catholic Worship.*

1. Seating. Here we most often take our cue from theaters, where it is important only that people see one focal point. But at liturgy it is important that people see each other also (more than backs of heads), that no one feel too removed from what is being done (for we are all doing it together), and that there be some freedom of movement. Rather than pews, the bishops speak of "benches or chairs" which "should be so constructed and arranged that they maximize feelings of community and involvement. . . . This means striving for a seating pattern and furniture that do not constrict people, but encourage them to move about when it is appropriate." (68) And the chairs used by the presider and other ministers "should be so constructed and arranged that they too are clearly part of the one assembly, yet conveniently situated for the exercise of their respective offices" (70).

2. Altar. "The altar, the holy table, should be the most noble, the most beautifully designed and constructed table the community can provide. It is the common table of the assembly, a symbol of the Lord, at which the presiding minister stands and upon which are placed the bread and wine and their vessels and the book." (71) Given this, the document suggests that the "holy table . . . should not be elongated, but square or slightly rectangular" (72). A fabric of good quality in design, texture and color can be used to cover the table, but other things—such as candles, cross, flowers—are best kept at some distance. (95, 72)

3. Books. "Any book which is used by an officiating minister in a liturgical celebration should be of a large (public, noble) size, good paper, strong design, handsome typography and binding. . . . The use of pamphlets and leaflets detracts from the visual integrity of the total liturgical action." (91)

The use of such pamphlets by the assembly is a good application of what has been said about judgments of hospitality, quality and appropriateness. The disposability of such monthly booklets hardly speaks well of the ministry these worshipers perform, hardly welcomes them to their prayer and invites them to participate with joy and dignity. They speak instead of the cheap and unimportant. "The hand stamp of the artist, the honesty and care . . . the pleasing form" that quality means are absent. Nor are such pamphlets in any way "appropriate." They do not serve the ritual action but impose upon it their own shabby standards.

4. Bread. It has been established that the bread used in the liturgy "appear as actual food," and that it should "be made in such a way that the priest can break it and distribute the parts to at least some of the faithful." (*General Instruction of the Roman Missal*, 282–283) Recipes for unleavened bread made from wheat flour are readily available; they yield a bread that looks and tastes and smells like real food.

5. Tabernacle. The church reserves the eucharistic bread "to bring communion to the sick and to be the object of private devotion." The tabernacle is to be in a "room or chapel specifically designed and separate from the major space . . . so that no confusion can take place between the celebration of the eucharist and reservation" (78). This chapel should offer easy access and should "support private meditation without distractions" (79).

Reflections

1. The material elements used at worship can enhance or cheapen a celebration. A fine altar cloth, a handsome set of cruets, an attractive chasuble can add a great deal to the character of worship. And a dingy baptismal font, a plastic candle, a poorly bound lectionary can weaken what might otherwise speak very powerfully to us. List some of the material elements used at worship. Think of the purpose each has. In your parish, how are the judgments of quality and appropriateness to be applied?

2. What participation aid is used? Is it worthy of the task?

Knowing What It Feels Like

We have seen something of the various elements that are important in our rituals; these have been grouped under the headings of Word, Movement, Music and Environment. These are very simple things; that is why they are capable of being used by us in so many different ways. They are the human activities, human arts, which can transcend their practical purposes (communicating information, getting the body around, etc.) to open to us our own spirit and all the mystery of existence.

The history of any group of believers, Jews and Christians included, shows how through generations the rituals change, evolve. The ways in which word, movement, music and environment are brought together adjust to express better the people's faith at a new time. Rituals are not created from a people's theology, as if someone sat down and thought: because we believe such and such about ourselves and such and such about God, let us have a way of praying, a ritual, which will first do this, then this, and so on. No, they spring from the faith, from the spirit: the spirit of gratitude leading to the lifting up of hands in the first morning light, the spirit of sorrow leading to ashes rubbed on the face. Words, sounds (music), gestures, objects—these are the stuff with which ritual takes shape and can live within the community. Thus, a community tells what its life means, and in turn strengthens that meaning.

Ritual is always closely associated with repetition. A people will give ritual expression to their beliefs around things which occur over and over. Among some people this will be the coming of the rainy season, or the gathering of harvest, or the full moon. There will also be the rituals which divide the time, as do the modern urban rites of TGIF (Thank God It's Friday). And there will be the daily rituals: of meals, of morning, of evening and night. Also, a people has rituals around the great events in life: birth, growing to adulthood, marriage, death. Rituals are to let the heart of the matter take expression in this particular moment, this particular situation. The repetition of the rituals, some yearly, some every few days, some every day, says much for how the various elements will take shape. We don't have Thanksgiving dinner every evening. We don't greet our spouse on the morning of the wedding anniversary in the way we do every other morning. We structure the rituals of everyday very simply, with freedom usually for them to take on some feeling from each day's uniqueness. And we often structure the less frequent rituals more elaborately.

When we come, then, to look at the Sunday eucharist or the celebration of baptism or funerals in a parish setting, or to look at the way a family's morning prayer or meal prayer might be done, we do so knowing that how word and movement and music and environment come together on any occasion for ritual should depend somewhat on the frequency of that ritual. When we come to view the whole working of ritual in a parish, we have first to know that we have a very great number of ways our tradition gives us to pray, some meant for everyday and some for once a year and some for once a lifetime. What each is to be like is very much dependent on good use of the richness of our tradition. If, for example, we know no other ritual than the eucharist, it will be extremely difficult to build a full life of faith, for we will have given up the greater part of our ritual heritage.

Our present problems—what keeps the liturgy from being the full work of the assembly it can be—have to do with all of this. We need strong but simple rituals for our everyday: the mornings and evenings and meals. We need other rituals, mainly the Sunday eucharist, that will pick up the mood of feasts and seasons and ordinary times. And within each Mass, we need a way of doing the ritual that has the dynamic, the rhythm, the flow that allows all of the elements—word, movement, music, environment—to work to the best possible advantage for our common praying.

Reflections

1. What are the daily, the weekly, the seasonal rituals of individuals or families through which we express our faith? How do we care for these? How do they care for us?

2. If this community had Sunday eucharist only twice a year, how would we sustain ourselves?

All Together: 2   # Rhythm and Pace

"Liturgy has its own structure, rhythm and pace: a gathering, a building up, a climax, and a descent to dismissal. It alternates between persons and groups of persons, between sound and silence, speech and song, movement and stillness, proclamation and reflection, word and action." (*Environment and Art in Catholic Worship*, 25) The potential of any liturgical celebration, the ability of those who are celebrating to pray fully through this ritual, depends on how well all these rhythms are put to the service of the prayer. From one point of view—all too often the only one around—the Mass or any other of our rituals is just a series of elements, like beads strung together: this one comes before that one but after that one. Most of us feel no sense of ownership. Do we engage in rituals which have been expressive of Christian prayer through the ages and are now entrusted to our hands so that we might pray well and have something to give those who follow? Or do we see our rituals as mechanical toys which, when wound, do their thing? This or that may change about such toys, but they remain mechanical.

When a liturgy is felt to be our prayer, the celebration of these people right here who stand in this tradition, then we begin to feel that these are not strung beads, but human actions. They are ours. It becomes possible to reflect on them. To name some of the elements in the rhythm, as the document quoted above does, helps this process: "It alternates . . . between sound and silence, speech and song, movement and stillness, proclamation and reflection, word and action" (25). Before we speak of the names we give these in a given ritual, whether it be "gospel," or "acclamation," or "blessing," we ought to be able to talk of them in terms of the kind of moment they are: that is, how do they come about? What makes them happen? How do people react?

1. Between sound and silence. In some religions, most of the ritual prayer is done in silence. Our tradition has insisted on the importance of silence, even within common prayer, while giving greater place to sound (spoken words, sung words, music, bells). But each gains its power from the other. Whenever, for example, there is reading of scripture, there is need for reflection and most often this is in silence. Too often in our liturgies the "hurry up" of society gets hold of us, and silence lasts only a few seconds. But this is exactly what destroys the rhythm, the back and forth of sound and silence. For prayer to happen, we need the silence to last so we can settle into it. Silence in common, the assembly and presider together, has a quality and a power that is missing in an individual's silent prayer. The assembly, in this silence, can sense what it means to be

praying together. The silence strengthens the words: like the pianist who was asked how he handled the notes so well and answered, "The notes I handle no better than many others, but the pauses between the notes—that is where the art resides."

2. Between speech and song. Some elements of prayer need the power of song by their very nature, especially the acclamations, litanies, and the psalms. Other parts because of their importance should be given special emphasis and reverence: important blessings, prayers (including the eucharist prayer). Still other elements, most especially the scriptures, are usually to be spoken. Finally, some moments have no words at all.

3. Between movement and stillness. Stillness is noticed by its absence. Even during a silence the minister may be looking through the book, cleaning the cups and plates; yet real silence does not happen without stillness. The movements— processions and gestures—need the balance of stillness.

Reverence has everything to do with the right pace, the right timing. When liturgy is the work of the whole person, the spirit with the body, then the beauty of praying makes for this reverent pace. The liturgical way of doing something is not efficient; hurrying liturgy can only make it seem foolish.

Reflections

1. Have you ever listened to the sound of silence as relatives stand over the crib of the first born? Or the grand silence of a wave approaching the shore? Or the silence of good friends? Or the expectant silence at an unveiling of art? Silence is the other half of our pulsating life. Listen for it in your prayer.

2. To be silent and still at liturgy is not easy when we live in a noisy, busy culture. But all the more reason our silence and stillness at worship can become a most treasured gift that helps put a necessary rhythm and pace into the liturgy, that helps us feel more at home with public prayer. Where in the Mass do we need silence? Why are people anxious at first when there is a long period of silence?

3. What can we do about the spirit of hurry?

Between Persons and Groups of Persons

The rhythm and the pace that are so important for good liturgy are not only matters of sound and silence, stillness and movement. There are also rhythms of the back and forth between people. This is not an arbitrary arrangement, worked out to be sure that everyone has something to do. It is the nature of the work.

In a ritual there are different things to be done. This in itself sets up a rhythm between the participants, for some will have developed their gifts for leading song, some for reading scripture, some for preaching, some for drawing all together and presiding. All of these are present first as members of the assembly, and they exercise their ministries in service of the whole assembly. The rhythm of the various kinds of ritual activities (singing, reflecting, listening, etc.) is only created as these people interact. But even as ministers develop their gifts for reading, leading song, leading prayer, they can be sensitive to the way the ministries support and complement one another.

The *Constitution on the Sacred Liturgy* of Vatican II noted: "In liturgical celebrations each person . . . who has an office to perform, should do all of, but only, those parts which pertain to that office by the nature of the rite and the principles of liturgy" (28). Certainly there are people who can read the scripture well and lead song well, people who can play the organ well and can preach well. Perhaps there are even people who can do everything well. That would not change the principle involved, for it is not aimed only at obtaining excellence in each ministry exercised within the liturgy but at this rhythm, this need for many persons to share their gifts, this sense that each person praying needs many others and deserves all. The prayer builds as lector, choir, cantor and presider interact with the assembly. And it is interaction: one is not active and the other passive. A passive assembly discourages good reading, good singing, good presiding. Attention, shown not only in volume of singing but in the eyes and posture, is the greatest spur to presider, cantor and lector to do their tasks well.

The liturgy of the word shows this rhythm among persons. A lector speaks the first scripture, then silence. Out of the silence, a cantor begins to sing a psalm and a song leader brings the whole assembly in on the simple refrain. A second reading from scripture needs another period of silence. Silence and stillness blossom in the gospel procession as deacon and acolytes move solemnly to the ambo and the whole assembly begins its alleluia acclamation. The gospel is announced and proclaimed and the homily is given, then the presider invites the prayers and a cantor leads the litany of intercessions.

In the eucharistic prayer, from "Lift up your hearts" to the "Amen" acclamation, there is a pattern of alternation between presider and assembly, prayer and acclamation, silence and speech and song. Other rites develop the pattern differently, but always sensitive to how each ministry needs the others.

We can appreciate something like this better by seeing a similar phenomenon at work in a very different context. Over the years, Johnny Carson of "The Tonight Show" has developed a number of routines which have elements of good rituals about them. In most of these, the audience (which is hardly the right word when speaking of the active part they take) and Ed McMahon are as important as Carson. There is no element of surprise: the comedy and enjoyment are in the repetition of the ritual, and—equally important to comedy and to prayer—in the timing.

Some of Carson's rituals are brief gestures: the little tap dance when the monologue is going poorly. Some are ritual questions the people are expected to know: "How *cold* was it?" A larger routine features Carson as Karnak the Magnificent. McMahon has his ritual introduction of the mysterious visitor from the East, Karnak enters, trips on the dais and has to remind McMahon not to touch his sacred person. Then McMahon does the speech about the hermetically sealed mayonnaise jar kept on Funk and Wagnalls' porch since noon. The people have their parts, times when they are expected to boo so that Carson may respond with a "curse," and times to cheer (as when McMahon announces: "I hold in my hand the last envelope . . ."). Everyone has a part, and it seems the more enjoyable for being as predictable as it is well executed. The context may be very different, but such examples tell us how important and natural is the "back and forth" in ritual.

Reflections

1. How aware are the various ministers of the rhythm and flow of the whole liturgy? Do they act on cues, or is the liturgy something integral, so that they act on a real sense for their own ministry?

2. Do the ministers act as if they are first of all members of the assembly called to serve that assembly?

Resources for *The Elements of Liturgy*

Environment and Art in Catholic Worship. (Bishops' Committee on the Liturgy.) Washington: USCC, 1978.

A fundamental document not only for matters of art and architecture but for understanding the basic importance of the assembly.

Fischer, Balthasar. *Signs, Words and Gestures.* New York: Pueblo Publishing Company, 1981.

Simple homilies by one of the authors of Vatican II's reform of the liturgy.

Funk, Virgil, ed. *Music in Catholic Worship: The NPM Commentary.* Washington: National Association of Pastoral Musicians, 1982.

A collection of articles dealing with individual sections of Music in Catholic Worship.

Music in Catholic Worship and *Liturgical Music Today.* (Bishops' Committee on the Liturgy.) Washington: USCC, 1983.

The 1972 statement, Music in Catholic Worship, *is the foundation for pastoral music.*

Who Does the Liturgy?

Ritual is the deed of people. We come with what we have: needs and gifts. In the great rituals of our tradition, the eucharist especially, the various moments—the scriptures to be read, psalms to be sung, communion to be shared—call for many different gifts. Good ritual is not magic, not automatic. It needs what all of us together can give.

Who Does the Liturgy?

The words "ministry" and "minister" occur more and more frequently. We hear, for example, of ministry to the sick, ministers of communion, the ministry of the deacon. These words help us understand how we relate to one another in the church community. Reflection on the scriptures and saints has impressed on many that there are many ministries in the church. And in every case, the one who ministers (to the sick, to those in prison, etc.) is also being ministered to.

When we speak then of ministry in the liturgy, of the various liturgical ministers such as the acolyte and the usher, we have a notion of how various members of the church take on specific tasks. We also get some sense that these tasks are in service to the whole community. As *Environment and Art in Catholic Worship* says: "God does not need liturgy; people do, and people have only their own arts and styles of expression with which to celebrate" (4). In our need for liturgy, for good rites done together, we offer our skills in this or that art so that the liturgy may be beautiful and strong. This is all that we have: this use of ourselves is ministry. Each minister—usher or cantor or homilist—emerges from the community. It is there, in the church itself, that we find what ministry means. It is basically the way Christians are, the way they behave. Eugene Walsh has developed this thought:

> We readily make ministry equivalent to "service." Indeed this has been a step forward, but I maintain we must have yet a radically different view of what ministry really is. Henry Nouwen offers the clearest insight into this new view when he insists that to minister does not mean "do things for" people, but rather "to be with" them. To minister, at its deepest level, means "to be present" to others. It means to care for others enough that you are willing to "be with" them, to keep on "paying attention" to them, to keep on staying in attendance to them. Personal presence comes first in effective ministry. If, while you are being present, there are also things to do for people, and services to offer, that is fine. But "doing for" is secondary to the being present. . . . Being a real minister becomes much more demanding. (*The Ministry of the Celebrating Community*)

This is especially helpful in understanding what happens in the liturgy. All of the ministries are most certainly about service. But that is true of most human rituals: to have a Fourth of July parade or a Thanksgiving dinner many people take on special roles and so serve the larger community. What distinguishes this ministering at our liturgy is the motivation: what comes first is not the worthy exercise of one's role, but that through this role one can be present, be there, be with others.

That is not to downplay the importance of doing the ministry well. Too often we have acted as if good will made people capable of any ministry. In fact, each ministry calls for very definite qualities, qualities which in most cases may be present and recognizable in a person and which can then be developed as the specific ministry is learned. These ministries are functions of the rituals we celebrate: they are not offices or ranks around which we build our prayer. Rather, liturgical ministries develop naturally from the common prayer itself as ways for the worthy presence of word, music, movement, environment and the patterns that these take.

As we go now to speak of the various specific ministries, we naturally have in mind the Mass as our most familiar community ritual. However, ministries are part of every gathering for prayer: morning prayer, the recitation of the rosary, the sacrament of reconciliation. We look at each rite and ask what it is that we are doing, what kind of a prayer would we want this to be, and so we know what are the ministries that will bring that about.

Reflections

Not everyone, of course, is capable of doing everything at liturgy. Some people are better suited for ushering, while others make good lectors and others ministers of communion. When the right person is paired with the right liturgical role, the ritual has its best chance of speaking to us, moving us to prayer. Good ministers breathe fresh life into rituals that breathe fresh life into all of us.

1. What liturgical ministries are needed in your community?
2. How can all the different liturgical ministries be coordinated?

The Assembly

Many things have to be done by many people for the liturgy on Sunday to be well celebrated in a parish. There is the priest, who is leader, presider. There is the lector who prepares and reads the scriptures. There is the leader of song. There is an organist or other musicians. There are those who help with the distribution of holy communion. There are the acolytes or servers. There are the ushers. Perhaps there is a deacon. There is the homilist (usually the presider or the deacon). And, behind the scenes but just as important, there are those who prepared the building, cleaning and decorating, those who wrote special parts of the liturgy for this Sunday, those who helped to coordinate the whole thing. And don't forget those who made the wine and baked the bread.

All of these have a ministry only because of the assembly—that's the name we use for everyone present. All of them are the assembly before being lector or usher. And what is the assembly?

What would a birthday party be like if no one sang "Happy Birthday"? Or what would a football game be like if no one cheered? Or what would your Christmas dinner be like if no one spoke to anyone else? Now all of these events, rituals, take special tasks: cake baking, cheerleading, sparking the conversation. But more than that, before all that, they need people who are anxious to lend voices, hands and even their hearts to make something happen, people who just want to be together and want to make that time a good time.

All the special ministries depend on what we all share: assembly. That seems to be quite a change from thinking about Sunday Mass as "going to church," or "attending Mass," as a time to say prayers while the priests and servers did the ceremonies of the liturgy. It seems to be quite a change from what people have in mind when they head straight for the back pews and try not to sit too close to anyone else. All of the "changes" of the last 20 years are not for God's sake, they are for the sake of the assembly: to make it possible for us to see our ministry and seize it. If liturgical renewal seems not to have gone very far, it is because we do not have all the answers for the assembly. Presiders, lectors, musicians can go only so far: the liturgy is done by the assembly.

The way it is done is very concrete. The first thing an assembly does is assemble: making one another welcome, taking places near the altar table and near to one another. Assemblies have to assemble, to get together: that is as essential to the ministry of assembly as a voice is to the ministry of song leader. The liturgy does not exist in a bubble somewhere untouched by whether or not we smile at one another, whether or not we sit together, whether or not we pay attention to each other. The liturgy is made possible and real or turned into a lifeless abstraction by such things.

This should not be forced. We are not asked to change our personality, just to show our faith. We have come for the praying of the community. It takes nothing away from the beauty of that prayer to say that it depends on being serious enough to be at home.

During the liturgy of the word, the assembly listens. Not reads, listens. Here and throughout the liturgy, except when a hymn is to be sung, there is no need for anything in the hands. That is what the assembly has to do to support the lector and the presider: give them our eyes, sign of our full attention. Here we also reflect on what has been read, in silence and in the psalm refrain. Here standing we join in a loud alleluia acclamation for the gospel. Here we listen to the homilist share reflections on the scriptures. And here we join in a litany of intercessions for all the world and the church universal.

Acclamation, during the eucharistic prayer, is the assembly's part. The acclamations are to come easily so that they can give voice to our praise and thanksgiving (which is what "eucharist" means).

Then the bread is broken, and the assembly shares the communion. Throughout the liturgy posture is an important part of the assembly's ministry: at communion, it is crucial. Here in the procession, in the reverence with which we hold ourselves and the bread and the cup, we experience the holy communion.

Very much is expected of the assembly: some of it spoken, some sung, some just in the eyes, some in the whole body. It makes all the difference.

Reflections

Have you previously thought that liturgy was for God? Are there practical dimensions to saying: "God does not need liturgy; people do"?

In the early 1900s the liturgical movement was gaining momentum. One sentence was repeatedly heard; it summarized well what the renewal of the liturgy was about: "Pray the Mass." Sounds like an innocent little piece of advice to us now, but it caused a great deal of discussion and sometimes resistance at the time. At the root of "Pray the Mass" was the renewal of the assembly's right and privilege and obligation to celebrate eucharist actively. For the early liturgical reformers, as for us today, participation meant more than keeping the assembly busy with singing and making responses. Active participation meant and still means that no one is a spectator. Everyone, by virtue of baptism, actively offers the one sacrifice of thanksgiving; everyone is a celebrant, though there is only one presider. The shape and quality of the worship then does not depend entirely upon the presider, musician, or liturgy planners, but upon the whole assembly. We must add ourselves to every act of worship.

The Presider

The word "presider," like the word "assembly," is new. It is often used instead of "celebrant" because all persons present are celebrants of the liturgy. But not all are presiders. The word has its drawbacks: too many associations with presiding at meetings, or judges presiding in the courtrooms. But it does point to what is most basic in this ministry: the priest-celebrant is to be a focus for the community's prayer. He is to know the liturgy thoroughly, to be completely at home with its rhythms—not so that he can take the part of a master of ceremonies, but so that he can give the assembly confidence and inspiration from his presence. The presider serves the assembly in the way he does the greeting, keeps the silences, listens to the scriptures, leads the prayers.

Until the reform of the liturgy mandated by Vatican II, the presider typically did several ministries. He had the deacon's ministry, the lector's, and sometimes a few others. We are only now learning what are the tasks and the skills *proper* to the presider. Basically, the presider has few spoken parts: to greet everyone and call them to prayer (in the introductory rites); to introduce and conclude the petitions; to lead the great eucharistic prayer; to lead the prayer after communion and to bless the assembly. The gospel reading and various invitations belong to the deacon, and the homily can be preached by the deacon. But if the spoken parts of the presider are few, it is to indicate their importance. When the presider takes on other roles, and perhaps adds commentary at various points throughout, then the parts that are truly proper to him begin to appear trivial. Presiding must not be understood as spoken parts alone: the breaking of the bread and sharing of communion, for example, are vital elements in the presider's role.

The qualities that would make for a good presider include the following:

● A sense that he is a member of the assembly. This is basic: the presider belongs as everyone else there belongs, a baptized Christian come to praise and thank the Lord. That shows in the plainest ways: if he sings when the assembly sings (hymns, acclamations, refrains); if he listens when the assembly listens and keeps silent reflection with the assembly; if his manner is that of a friend.

● Grace in movement, reverence in gesture. The manner matters. It matters at a cocktail party, at the checkout counter of the supermarket, in a cab. The words can be the same, but what one is doing with hands and eyes and the whole body communicates that person's presence (or lack of it) and attitude toward us. If the presider says, "The grace and peace of our Lord Jesus Christ be with you," and his eyes are not on us, his arms are not open in greeting, then he is not presiding. If he says, "Lift up your hearts," while turning pages in the book, no hearts will be lifted. If he handles the bread and wine mechanically at the table and at communion, all the words in the world cannot draw us to the mystery that is present. No movement of the presider will be neutral: how he sits, walks, extends the peace, blesses, offers communion, all can build up the prayer. Such a grace in movement, reverence in touch, is not acquired just for the liturgy: it is honest reflection of a person's life, of one's sense for the presence of God in all creation.

• A voice for the prayer. Grace and reverence are important here also: how are they found in the tone, volume, pace and cadences of the speech? Much of what the presider speaks, especially in the eucharistic prayers, are familiar words. The challenge is not to find a way to make them sound somehow new each time, but rather to find a way of speaking that fits this occasion of great thanksgiving, that catches the mood of the prayer in the very sound itself. This is why chanting the prayer texts can be effective.

• A sense of pace. Timing can be everything: not because liturgy is entertainment, but because it is human. Why is the same joke funny when told by one person and flat when told by another? A sense for pace is something some have and some need to work hard to obtain. At prayer, it means a feeling, a sensitivity, for the involvement of the community: knowing the right moment to begin and to end each element in the ritual.

In everything, the assembly needs to support the presider: through our own attention in posture and eyes, through our own reverence in gesture (as at communion), through our own strong speech.

(Note: In this section and the next the masculine pronoun has been used because, in the present discipline, presiders and deacons at the eucharist in the Roman Catholic church are male. However, what has been said applies also to other liturgies when the presider may be male or female: e.g., liturgy of the hours, communion services.)

Reflections

At times, each of us is a presider. This might be at a party, at a family meal, on Thanksgiving Day. Reflect on what it feels like, what qualities it calls forth.

The one who is probably most sensitive to the assembly's ministry is the presider. Celebrants often remark that every Mass congregation has its own personality. Some congregations are always responsive, making the presider more responsive in turn. At some Masses the congregation is so dispirited that the presider feels like the only one worshiping and consequently finds it hard to be a spirited presider.

The Deacon

The renewal of the ministry of deacon within the church has not been primarily related to the liturgy. Rather, permanent deacons have become involved in every aspect of the church's work and presence. Since the liturgy is not simply another field of church work, but is where the church is entirely itself, at home, expressing its whole life, those who are deacons have traditionally taken a role in the worship service.

The deacon is ideally the one who is to have a grasp on the order of the entire service. This can be seen in the way the deacon addresses various instructions to the assembly concerning the peace greeting, the acclamations, the dismissal. This is also clear from the deacon's place beside the presider. Without a deacon, the presider gives most of these instructions, and the acolytes are (ideally anyway) responsible for a good sense of the flow of the liturgy. But presider and acolytes do these things not as their own, but as necessary in the deacon's absence.

One characteristic of a deacon, then, would be this sense for the dynamics of the ritual, for the proper ordering of words and movements and music toward good strong prayer. In this, the deacons must know how to speak simply and honestly to the assembly; the deacon's hospitality here takes shape in words of invitation which are to be few but warm and addressed directly to the people.

The deacon is to read the gospel. Deacons must have the skills of a lector and the presence to make the procession with the book to the lectern a physical announcement and acclamation of the good news.

The deacon is to address the assembly at the prayers of intercession. These also are invitations: "In peace, let us pray to the Lord." It is the assembly that actually makes the prayer in the response, "Lord, hear our prayer," or, "Lord, have mercy." Since it is nearly always better to sing a litany such as this, the intercessions are often led by the cantor, but when the deacon is able to sing them well, they belong to this ministry. The formulating of these prayers may be the work of the deacons since their ministry brings them into close touch with the needs of the whole church, the society, the poor and especially the needs of the local community.

Frequently in this ministry, the deacon will be carrying and handling various things: the thurible when incense is used, the wine vessels, the communion plate and the bread, the gospel book. The quality of reverence and the sense for pace are essential in these movements. The whole manner must say how much it matters that there is a book, that there is the sweet smelling incense, that there is bread and wine.

The deacon needs to be comfortable in directing the common

prayer. The deacon may preside at morning or evening prayer, at the giving of holy communion apart from Mass, at weddings and burials, at various other devotions. The deacons of a community can be those who by example show that the skills of public prayer are learned through the smaller gatherings, in the prayer of the home, in personal prayer. In this as in their whole ministry they have the possibility of breaking down images of the church which set clergy and laity in opposition, and establishing images where the ordained are ordained for the service of all.

Reflections

Who are the deacons in other human communities? In schooling, in recreation programs, in political parties? When do we see the role of the deacon handled well in a nonchurch setting?

Deacons are still new to most congregations. That means that their role, which is never exclusively liturgical, is still developing. They are rooted in service and their ministry at the altar should be a reflection of that service. This will be especially evident as the deacon keeps an attitude of such service in all the liturgical actions: never dominating, never overpowering the presider or the other ministers.

By service in community, the deacon can be instrumental in developing a good liturgical spirit. The deacon's love for the word of God and ability to show others how to pray are examples of this ministry.

1. How do deacons minister at the Mass?
2. Are there any avenues of liturgical service that should be recommended to the deacons?
3. How much a part of the planning for liturgy should deacons have?

The Homilist

In many of our liturgies, and especially at the eucharist, we have the tradition of public reflection on the scriptures that have been read. This homily is normally the task of the presider, sometimes of the deacon. The preparation involves (at least) ". . . prayer, the scripture study, the familiarity with the life of the community, and the skill of writing or outlining for oral discourse" (Robert Hovda in *Strong, Loving and Wise*).

Those are time and energy consuming requirements. They point toward a very special way of speaking, a way that is well rooted in Jewish and Christian forms of worship. The homily is not simply an explanation of the scriptures, the fruit of research into the best scholarship. Nor is it the drawing of a moral from the scriptures, nor using the scriptures to back up the latest need for school support or abortion law reform. Nor is the homily a great literary creation "from nothing": the scriptures and eucharist are its beginning and its ending.

The homilist knows how to reflect on the scriptures, how to stand before the scriptures. This requires knowledge of the books, the authors, the times, the way they have been used by the church. But all that may be only clearing the way for the homily to take shape. The homilist is not first of all one who can interpret the scriptures, but one who can be interpreted by them, who can put life and struggle and joy before these texts and share what takes shape. For most, that is terribly hard work. And it is only the beginning, for the homilist must make the work interesting. That is what it is all about.

"The first requirement for preaching interestingly is not to use too many words to say simple things. This is not a matter of the length of time spent in speaking. The long homily can be interesting, the short homily dull. It is a matter of how explicit, how wordy we are in getting a thing said. If we examine the teachings of Jesus, we see how economical he was with words. When he was not sparing of words, as in the allegorical explanations appended to some of the parables, it turns out that the author was not Jesus but the evangelists. They are less effective teachers than he in their attempt to make everything perfectly clear. They multiply words in a dull way, causing their readers to lose interest rather than grow in it.

"This means that the preacher must put restraints on himself before he begins, to ensure that he won't say too much. He has to know, not simply where he's going to stop but where he's going to stop a dozen times, even in individual sentences.

"Our Lord's genius in presenting an idea—let's say the idea of compassion—is that he went at it from many different angles. He would make a short thrust, an allusion, then back away. He would tell a story about a compassionate act, and leave it there. The story did the job for him; he never moralized. In five, eight, ten ways he would tease his listeners into reflecting on what it meant to be compassionate. The one thing you can't accuse Jesus of is beating an idea to death.

"He was uncanny at appealing to people's experience. They knew how commercial dealing was carried on. They knew it was full of crookedness and self-interest. He didn't linger on that, stopping to deplore it at great length. He just drew on it as an example of the way things were, to move on to deeper matters. If just one listener decided to turn his or her value system around, specific abuses in the world of business or trade would be tackled soon enough. Jesus was never painfully obvious in his teaching. He went to the ethical jugular every time: that basic self-interest that makes living for others an impossibility, unless there is radical change." (Gerard Sloyan in *Liturgy*, May 1974)

The homilist's ministry begins in being one of the persons at prayer in this community, in knowing the people and their concerns. They, in turn, support the homilist: by giving attention, by serious reflection on what is said, by thoughtful criticism.

Reflections

The role of homilist is probably the most difficult of all liturgical ministries. In addition to basic training, there is a constant need to prepare every time one preaches. This preparation may take a great deal of time. It will always take prayer and sensitivity to the mind of the assembly. A homilist may improve by attending preaching workshops, spending more time in prayer and study of scripture, but the assembly can be a great source of help to the homilist. We have to find ways for the congregation to express spiritual needs more clearly and to offer feedback in helpful ways. The homilist in turn must learn to seek advice and listen carefully.

1. It's easy to complain about poor homilies, but is it possible to say why they are poor?
2. Would it make any difference if we dropped the homily every Sunday?
3. How can a liturgy team and homilist work together?

The Minister of Music

A number of ministries in the liturgy deal directly with music: organists and other instrumentalists, choir directors and members, cantors and leaders of song, members of small ensembles (no longer simply classified as folk groups.) The development of all these is witness to our awareness that good liturgy will be musical liturgy: musical because that is the only way that such essential rites as the acclamations and litanies can be done by the assembly, and musical because the special ministries of instrumentalists and choirs not only support the assembly but greatly enhance the processions, times of reflection, and much more.

As parishes have grown in their awareness of what music can be in the liturgy, they have been inclined to coordinate all the parish musicians through a minister of music. The title may vary, but the job description has come to include the following elements: director of choir, in charge of training cantors and leaders of song, responsible for coordinating all music with the planning of the parish liturgy committee. It is understood in all these phases of the work that the goal is the musical liturgy of a singing assembly.

The minister of music is charged to develop in others the ways in which their art will be integral to the liturgy. The musical qualifications for this ministry will often be present before the person has had an opportunity to develop that necessary sense for the liturgy. This may have to be acquired gradually through reading, workshops, summer institutes, experiences of good musical liturgy in other parishes.

In addition, the minister of music must work well with other musicians and with the various musical groups. Quality, in any style that can serve the prayer of the people, should be the criterion. The minister's good imagination will serve to integrate good musical abilities.

The minister of music will work closely with all those involved in liturgical roles, especially the cantors, leaders of song, organists, choir members and small ensembles.

Cantor. This ministry is to sing the verses of psalms and sometimes of other songs. The assembly sings the refrains. The cantor needs musical abilities and a good sense for the way we pray through music. The cantor's singing is very much like the presider's leading of prayer: the cantor needs to enter into the psalms as prayers just as the presider enters the eucharistic prayer. What the cantor does *is* prayer.

Leader of song. Often this will be the same person as the cantor. The leader of song assists the assembly in their hymns and acclamations. This minister must work most closely with the organist, and must have a good sense for when leadership and support are needed, and when the assembly can function quite well on its own.

Organist. The principal role of the organist is to lead the assembly's song through vigorous and energetic playing. Secondary roles include accompanying cantor and choir and providing instrumental music to reinforce the mood of the celebration. By steady tempo, bright registration and authoritative playing, the organist must lead, stimulate and inspire song rather than accompany or follow along.

Choir. Rehearsed and more skilled than the assembly, the choir should enrich and embellish the community song. Ideally, there is more than one parish choir: adult mixed, children's, youth, etc. The choir does not replace the congregation, but enriches the assembly's singing with artistic beauty and musical complexity.

Small ensemble. This is another way of doing the tasks of choir, organist and leader of song. Skill and liturgical understanding are presupposed. There are great possibilities here for talented and creative leaders. The use of various instruments can provide color and prevent monotony (e.g. string bass gives a bottom to the music much like the pedal on the organ). The group is a leader of prayer with the constant challenge to turn performance into prayer.

Reflections

Can you imagine an unenthusiastic cheerleader? Or a rock concert without amplifiers? Or a birthday party at which the celebration song is begun with a whispering, dirge pace?

What enthuses you to participate in song?

Many well intentioned attempts at congregational singing have been frustrated by problems of poor acoustics, inadequate sound system or instrument. A live room (with echo) is best for amplifying congregational response. A sound engineer should be consulted in obtaining a sound system that is suitable both for use by the cantor and the lectors and homilists. The organ, whether pipe or electronic, must be designed to fit the building. Unless it has adequate resources for the size of the room, it will not be able to stimulate congregational song.

Some congregations only have a hymn board to lead them, some have a lector who might also be a commentator and who may not have a very good sense of music. But congregations that really sing have been taught to sing; they have been encouraged to sing through enthusiastic, good direction.

1. What value would a minister of music be to your community?
2. How can the organist and the leader of song encourage the assembly to sing?

The Lector

The presider or deacon usually reads the gospel and so must be, in every sense, an adequate lector. But someone other than the presider does the first readings because this task requires great preparation and the assembly benefits from hearing different voices.

The lector is the storyteller of the community. Like the elders of a tribe, the lector publicly tells the story that identifies us. As Catholics, we have far to go before we feel ourselves to be immersed in this story, to know the scriptures deeply. In this the lector is to be a leader, for before there can be a powerful telling of the story, the teller has to plunge into it, learn about it, know the characters and times and places. The lector is to know these not as Bible history, but as the story which gives meaning to our lives, the story which "tells us" much more than we tell it. We generally know at once when a lector has failed to prepare a particular reading from the scripture, but we seem also to have a sense for something more important: whether the person reading is at home in the scriptures, loves them, prays with them.

Like the presider, the lector needs a sense that the ministry is first to be part of the assembly. Also like the presider, the lector needs grace in movement (in carrying the book of the scriptures in procession, and in going to and from the lectern; even in standing in silence after the reading).

But the special gifts and skills of the lector have to do with drawing everyone into the scriptures. The direct preparation for this is thorough familiarity with the reading. The lector, many days before the liturgy, begins to let the reading loose, tries out its language, lets the language play back and forth in the mind. The lector lets the reading into daily life: a verse that can run through the mind, go in and out with breathing. At some point it becomes important to read the scriptures that surround this particular reading, to get the context, the environment. With several readings of the scripture, spaced through the week, the lector becomes more and more free of the printed page; as a sense for how this passage is to be read develops (where to put emphasis, where to pause, where to be loud and where soft, where to be fast and where slow), so does the ability to "read" with only an occasional glance at the printed words. Then the lector's whole manner can be directed to the listeners. Lectors should never fear to "overdo" in this regard; it is simply not that likely to happen.

This preparation will also show what the mood of this reading, this part of our story, is to be. A narrative from Kings is one mood, a selection from the Law in Deuteronomy another, an angry outburst from Jeremiah another. You do not read Dickens' novels, the Declaration of Independence, or the sermons of Martin Luther King, Jr., in the same manner. But that does not mean that one is dull in comparison with another: they are to be interesting in different ways.

Within the liturgy, the lector also needs that sense for pace: waiting to begin until people have "settled" and are ready—and then making sure that they are grabbed by the first words, by their sound as much as by their content. Pace within the reading is a matter of expression, interpretation. After a pause, the final "This is the word of the Lord" must be said in such a way as to invite the "Thanks be to God" of the assembly.

Reflections

The lector is a lover of the word who truly wants to communicate the news to the community.

1. Sometimes even a good lector can have a hard time because of poor lighting, poor sound system, or poorly printed text. Check these essentials.
2. What is your training program? Is it ongoing?
3. What resources are available to the lector in your parish to improve their reading and understanding of the scriptures?

The Acolyte: Servers

When a group of any size meets to celebrate the liturgy, someone needs to take responsibility for freeing the presider from various details so he may give full attention to presiding. The various tasks include: assisting with the book of prayers (sacramentary) when the presider needs to read from it; helping to set the altar table with the bread and wine; helping to share the communion, both bread and cup; setting the plates and cups aside after communion and, after Mass, making sure they are clean; taking care of the candles, incense and processional cross.

Generally these tasks are taken on by two different groups of ministers: the servers (often youngsters), and the ministers of communion. Here we discuss the former and in the next section the latter.

Though we have most often thought of servers as children who simply memorize their movements and words and add solemnity to the procession in and out, the need of the presider and of the whole assembly is not for such purely mechanical help and sanctuary dressing. The need is for someone who knows the order of the liturgy thoroughly, can anticipate each moment and need, and can meet these with grace and reverence. This is not a job description for a child. As long as we continue with children in this ministry, we can only try to work with them until they have a total familiarity with the ordinary order of the service, and have some sense of how to move, carry things, and keep stillness and silence. An advantage to allowing children to take this role is simply engaging them in liturgy, but we should have some hesitation about the judgment such an "advantage" makes on our whole approach to the liturgy.

It is best a ministry for adults and teen-agers. In most cases, only one server is needed during the liturgy itself: to hold the book for the presider, to help with the bread and wine. The processions at beginning and end, and usually the gospel, might use additional servers to carry candles and incense and cross. The seating for acolytes should be off to one side, not beside the presider.

Since servers are concerned with books and other objects that are used in liturgy, they need a sense for the way things are to be handled. What these things make possible is central to our liturgy: the reading from the book, the eating of the bread and drinking from the cup, the burning of candles and of incense. In their making and their use, these things are worthy of reverence. Obviously, the parish that has no concern for the quality of these objects (an extreme: imitation candles, plastic forms with invisible candles inside; missalettes and sheets of paper instead of books) cannot ask the servers to do their task and handle these with reverence.

Servers, whatever their age, should be seen singing, listening, keeping good silence. They are to model the activity of the assembly. It is difficult to imagine people taking their prayer seriously and wholeheartedly when those who have special roles regard attentiveness as unimportant.

The question of vestments for servers is often raised, as it is for lectors and ministers of communion. The answer is not based on any matter of rank, of somehow incorporating more people into the clergy. Rather, it is a question of what is fitting, what will help the assembly's prayer. It should be clear that the ministers are first of all members of the assembly. Vestments for the presider, for the deacon, sometimes for other ministers, are appropriate when they help the prayer. Simplicity and beauty should characterize vestments as all other objects used in the liturgy. In general, the vestment that belongs to all ministers in our tradition is the alb, a robe covering the entire body. "The more these vestments fulfill their function by their color, design and enveloping form, the less they will need the signs, slogans and symbols which an unkind history has fastened on them." (*Environment and Art in Catholic Worship*, 94)

Reflections

Respect is the attitude an assembly expects in those who touch beautiful things or help during solemn movements. Respect: *re-spect*, to look back, to look again. The definition indicates a learning and a *re-membering* process. It calls forth a sense of wonder. What is respectful about books? Vessels? Water? Incense?

We put acolytes into service because we see a need for them. When we ask members of our congregation to serve as acolytes, we ought to make clear what the ministry entails. And they must be trained for these responsibilities. The training ought to include not only a careful modeling of *what* they will be expected to do at liturgy, but *how* they are to perform this service. Besides the mechanics, the servers should have a good sense of the liturgy as a whole, so they can be prepared for the expected and for the unexpected. They ought to be especially sensitive to the way in which they can influence the atmosphere of prayer by their presence in the sanctuary.

1. What are acolytes expected to do in your parish?
2. How does the ministry practically relate to the other liturgical ministries?

The Acolyte: Ministers of Communion

The acolyte's ministry has to do with helping. Those who take on this particular part of that ministry, for holy communion, are helping the whole community. Primarily, they make it possible for the communion rite to take place in a length of time that is not out of proportion to the whole liturgy. This is not a matter of efficiency, but a recognition that the meaning of the holy communion cannot be separated from its experience in the ritual. When "going to communion" takes a long time, and so the eating and drinking *together* is not experienced, then the communion rite loses its association with the eucharistic prayer and the breaking of the bread. The number of ministers of communion needed, therefore, is determined by the number of communicants at a Mass, and by whether or not the cup is also to be shared.

These ministers come forward from the assembly, but at a moment when this movement will not be a distraction, competing for attention with the breaking of the bread or the Lord's Prayer. They can come forward after the Amen of the eucharistic prayer, and be present at the table for the entire communion rite; or they can come forward at the peace greeting, perhaps greeting people with the peace as they approach the table and take their places. At the table they join in singing the "Lamb of God," a litany which is meant to last as long as it takes to break the bread and prepare the cups.

After the presider has invited all to communion, "Happy are they . . . ," the ministers should go as soon as possible to share the bread and cup with the rest of the assembly. It is unwise to take a great deal of time with the communion of the ministers themselves (or of concelebrants), lest it appear like two communion services. When this is a problem, the ministers might receive communion after everyone else. After communion, they do not return to the altar table, but take the vessels to the side. After the liturgy, they may return to clean the vessels carefully and put them away. (The preparation of bread, wine and vessels before Mass and the cleaning afterwards may be the responsibility of the sacristan, or this could be a duty of the ministers of communion.)

Those selected for this ministry should have, or soon acquire, that grace in movement and reverence in touch which are to characterize all who minister before the assembly. Reverence in touch is especially important for ministers of communion since their whole work is to take in hand the vessels of bread and of wine and to share them with everyone. A true reverence for what they carry is to be seen and felt by all: not a false humility, but a strong sense of joy and delight in the sharing of the

Lord's body and blood. That can translate to how the plate is picked up and carried, how the minister stands, how the cup or plate is later returned to a side table. It may be as simple a matter as using both hands, rather than one, to carry the plate or cup.

Most of all, the minister of communion must be a person who can put reverence into practice when giving the bread and cup to others. "The moment of communion is one that should be seized by both the minister and the communicant. . . . This is one moment when attention should be individual and total. The eyes of the minister should meet the eyes of the communicant. The minister says the words of the formula *to* the person (not to the air). . . . In placing the holy bread on the palm of the communicant's hand, the minister will touch the hand. And the same will be true of the ministry of the cup. *Eye contact, direct address, touching!* All are a communion of persons in the Lord. . . . This means that there can be no rush. One can minister communion with reverence and dignity and personal attention and still keep the procession moving steadily. But it cannot be done in haste, or with absent-mindedness, or with frantic searchings of the approaching processional lines." (*It Is Your Own Mystery.*) Some parishes have helped this happen by assigning four ministers to each station: one holds the plate of bread, another is then free to give all attention to taking bread and giving it to the communicants; the other two ministers stand a little distance away, each with a cup of wine. Sometimes one additional minister is needed to go from station to station refilling wine cups.

Those who are to take on this ministry must, above all else, be individuals who know how to be truly present to others in the moment they have. They are not dispensing machines, but brothers and sisters in this very body and blood they are sharing. They not only speak their own faith in saying "The body of Christ," but they call forth the faith of the communicant.

Reflections

"Eye contact, direct address and touching" are part of the experience of sharing. At what sharing times in your life is this true? Think about homecomings, farewells, times of forgiveness, times of tragedy. Can the sharing of bread and cup be anything less than an intimate moment?

By his or her eyes, smile, and gentle serving of bread and cup, the minister of communion tells us this is a very special event. The minister can make us feel good to be present at this feast, can remind us that our communion with the Lord is also communion with one another.

1. Do you sense any difference in receiving communion from one minister to another? Describe a good minister of communion.
2. What are your criteria for selecting ministers of communion?

The Usher

The usher does one thing that everyone there is to be doing: welcoming everyone and offering hospitality. Ushers are the community's way of being sure that this happens, being sure that the first face everyone sees at church is smiling, being sure we get the idea that here people are expected to sit together, being sure that strangers are welcomed and made to feel at home. Those are things everyone in the assembly has some responsibility for, but the usher is one who takes this responsibility most seriously.

Yet somehow this work often separates ushers from the rest of the assembly. Welcoming may in fact be ignored altogether, and seating may be done in a very mechanical way more characteristic of the theatre or sports event than the Christian community. And ushers have been notorious for habits which, during the liturgy, seem to say that they are too important or busy to be concerned about singing or praying or keeping silence with the assembly.

It is the usher's ministry to greet people warmly, to introduce strangers, to help people sit together, to pass out hymnals when necessary, to care for any needs (if someone gets sick, or other emergencies), to take up the collection, to help with good order at communion, to distribute bulletins and such in the course of saying goodbye to everyone or to direct people to coffee in the parish hall.

As with all the ministries, the question to ask is: What kind of a person is best suited to do these things well? Two things would seem to stand out.

First, the man or woman who would be an usher must be one with a sense for liturgical prayer. If a person has experience of how this kind of prayer is not just an audience watching while a priest says Mass, then that person has one qualification to be an usher. Such a person will not want to see people unwelcomed, spread out over the room. And that person will not want to do anything other than enter into the assembly's prayer during the liturgy itself. No chatter in the back, no disturbing walks up and down the aisles to look for places for latecomers, no counting heads or money. Just joining in prayer.

And second, the one who would be an usher must have a gift for hospitality. Like the ability to read well aloud, or the ability to lead singing, there will probably be something obvious about this, something to build on. The usher should be comfortable at welcoming the regulars and the strangers. If a warm greeting for a large number of persons comes hard, or if there is great difficulty recalling names, then perhaps this person belongs in a different ministry. Many parishes have discovered that they have no shortage of people who have the exact gifts needed for ushering, but until now they had not even considered these people: because they are women, or are elderly, or are teen-agers.

Everything else about being an usher can be easily learned by people who have a sense for the prayer of the assembly and a sense of hospitality. Such people will, in fact, be the best ones to take up a collection, to help those who don't feel well, to distribute the bulletins, to take care of any needs special to the day (a procession, a first communion). In many cases, it is simply a matter of the present ushers never having the ministry opened up to them. In other cases, they may be able to continue to do the parts of the ministry they like and understand, such as taking up the collection and handing out bulletins, while others are added to exercise more of the ministry of hospitality.

Reflections

Have you ever noticed the difference in your feeling: when a hostess seats you in a restaurant you are experiencing for the first time, and when a hostess recognizes you as a regular at a frequently shared place?

Have you ever been invited to a gathering, knowing you may know only the one who invited you? What a relief when someone reaches out to welcome you!

We men and women who are active in the parish may not pay much attention to the ushers because we feel pretty much a part of the community. We may not feel the need to be welcomed. We may not have to be shown to a front seat. We are probably easily recognized by others and made to feel at home. But most of the congregation isn't so easily recognized, nor so quickly made to feel at home. Maybe we should visit another parish where we are not so well known and see if we feel welcomed. We have to put ourselves into the shoes of the shy, the unpracticing, the infrequent worshiper to get a sense of what we want to look for in our ushers.

1. How do your expectations for ushers match their own perception of the role? Are they clear about their responsibilities?
2. What are the criteria for choosing ushers in your parish?
3. Is a training period for ushers feasible?

The Commentator

In the first years of liturgical reform, the commentator was introduced to explain the changes and help people feel comfortable with the English liturgy. Often this has continued, like many other things in liturgy, long beyond the need for it. Explanations and directions are no longer needed: in part because everyone now has some feeling for the rhythms of the liturgy, and in part because more and more people realize that ". . . if the signs need explanations to communicate faith, they will often be watched instead of celebrated" (Music in Catholic Worship, 8).

Is there any need for a minister other than the lector, presider, deacon and cantor or leader of song to speak to the assembly? There are only two elements which do not belong to one of these other ministries: the welcome at the beginning of the liturgy, and the announcements. Beyond these two things, the commentator may give the needed information on what is to be sung in the absence of a leader of song, and may be needed to read or sing the verses of the responsorial psalm. In the absence of cantor and deacon, the commentator may read or sing the intercessions in the prayer of the faithful.

The words of welcome and the announcements make this ministry closest to that of the usher: it is part of the hospitality, part of the introducing, the welcoming, and part of the sharing of the household's news. The talents that are called for in this "commentator" (whoever it is that introduces and makes the announcements) are not so much those of the lector as they are those of a good usher: outgoing, friendly and smiling, a good host. The commentator brings these in the voice and in the facial expression. The commentator's will generally be the first voice the assembly hears: it would be well then if it conveyed not only welcome but security.

This welcoming is the goal of any comment made before the liturgy. This introduction is not meant to give a summary of the scriptures or historical background on the feast or season. Whatever is said, the goal is to welcome, sincerely welcome, and to put people at their ease. That is something that is done through the manner and tone much more than through the words. The words can be saying, "Good morning" (and waiting for a response), can give the names of the ministers, can alert people to anything special for the day, can tell about the opening hymn. But it is the way it is said that gets the job done. This introduction can help set the tone for the entire prayer together. At its conclusion, people want to sing, want to pray together. Anything said should not only help form community, it should be conscious of the season or the feast. The commentator should also consider how people feel as they come to this particular Mass on this particular day.

The announcements, coming just before the blessing and the dismissal, are like what happens before the end of a family meal, just as people go their separate ways. Someone says, "Oh, don't forget about Uncle Frank's birthday next week," and someone else says: "I need help with the dishes!" Parishes have other ways of giving detailed information to people. The announcements are just to hit on a few crucial family matters, particularly those that show the kind of social actions which flow from this eucharist.

Reflections

Imagine yourself trying to stop the action and conversation at your family meal five or six times in order to tell the people what will be happening next during the meal. A community familiar with ritual wants to experience it, not hear what they will experience.

It is inevitable that we will use words at liturgy. But just exactly *what* needs to be said and *who* should say it and *when* are crucial questions.

Sometimes we work backwards. Our parish may have commentators and so we feel obligated to write comments for them rather than beginning with a need to say something and then finding the right minister to say it.

In the developing liturgy of the church, the liturgical ministries develop too. We have to be free enough to see some ministerial roles change, some added and some eliminated.

1. If comments are made at liturgy, who prepares the text? How?
2. At what times are there comments? Do all serve the work of prayer through the ritual?

Writers

Those who minister by writing should take into account all that has been said of the commentator, for any basic introductory comments and sometimes the announcements will come from the writers.

Writers will also have responsibility for creating or choosing texts for several other elements in the liturgy. These would include:

The penitential rite. Three forms of this rite are offered in the sacramentary. These are intended to suggest ways in which this rite can be done and to offer examples of the words that can be used. Depending on the season of the year, planners will give more or less emphasis to the penitential rite. There will often need to be some composing of texts, or some selection from existing texts. It is most important that those doing this work be aware that the penitential rite is not an examination of conscience, nor even an act of contrition, but praise of God's unfailing mercy and love for us. It may be shaped by the mood of the season, but is not a "mini-homily." It has most often the form of a litany and needs to do its work with few words.

Introductions to the readings. These should be used only when they are needed to set the stage: to place the reading in some context, to identify a place or character. Even so, they should not appear as mere information, but as invitations to get involved in the reading. Introductions should hardly ever be used and should never summarize the reading.

The prayers of intercession (or petitions, or prayers of the faithful). The writers should know that this prayer is a litany, and that a litany "works" because of the strong repetition of the refrain, and the rhythm of the leader's lines between the refrains. Ordinarily, litanies are sung. The refrain, the people's part, will be stronger if it is not changed from week to week; possibly it can be varied with the seasons. The refrain will be stronger if the words that lead into it, whether the whole is spoken or sung, have a pattern that tells the assembly to be ready. Writers do well to build a collection of beautiful intercessory prayers from various traditions, especially from the Byzantine liturgy, and to draw freely on these. The language is important: the flow of the words, the beauty of expression. The content is equally important: not so general that the thrust of the gospel in our lives is lost, not so particular that we lose sight of the universal needs. Often it will do to select a few petitions from those that have served well through many centuries, and to write one or two others that speak of immediate needs and reflect the mood of the days at hand. The language of scripture, and in particular of the scriptures of the current season, can be a source of words and phrases that help to shape these prayers. The prayers of intercession are always to give a sense for the support the churches give to one another throughout the world in our constant prayer, and a sense for the special responsibility we have to pray for those in power and for those who are poor and in any need, and finally to pray for this assembly as a community with its own special needs.

Invitations. The writers can help the presider and the deacon by suggesting forms for the invitations: the deacon's invitation for the assembly to join in the memorial acclamation and in the peace greeting, and the presider's invitation for all to come to the holy communion. As invitations, these should not ordinarily be read, so the writer's task is to suggest very brief forms that allow particular ministers to make these invitations very personal and direct. The deacon's words of dismissal at the end of the liturgy would come under this heading also.

Other texts. The writers may also be the ones to take responsibility for becoming thoroughly familiar with the sacramentary so that they can suggest the possible choices in texts for the preface, for the eucharistic prayer (there are four texts in the sacramentary, three others for Masses with children, two others for Masses where reconciliation has an important place), and for the final blessing.

Good writers are rather rare. No other kind should be used. Care for words—their power, their beauty—and patience in composing are essential. So is a sensitivity that guides the writer to use inclusive language at all times. This need not sound at all awkward. Awkwardness comes when, on the spot, the reader is adding "and she" to every "he," "or her" to every "his." Texts which are composed locally can be inclusive without being self-conscious.

Sacristans and Artists

These are ministers whose work and presence is known in the room and in the things that are seen and touched within the liturgy. Those who clean and polish as much as those who create vestments and hangings come from the assembly to care for specific needs: fashioning a place that helps people pray together. The two groups will need to stay very close in their thinking and in their work. Both need a vision of the overall task: an environment that is hospitable, welcoming, clean, human; an environment that is beautiful, that of itself points beyond to the awe and wonder that foster our prayer; an environment that is honest, the work of caring people.

These ministers should have a sense for the commonness of the objects that we use in our prayer. We are not a church that uses "cult objects" in order to pray. Our prayer does not depend on anyone manufacturing anything that is not also needed in the course of simple human life. We sit at benches and chairs; we place a good loaf of bread on a plate; we put wine in a cup; plate and cup rest on a table covered with some good fabric; we listen to scriptures read from a worthy book; we immerse new members of the community in ordinary water; we help to center our attention and prayer through burning candles and through vestments and hangings. But all of these—benches, bread, wine, table and cloth, book, water, candle, fabric—are things of everyday life. We sit, we eat bread and drink wine, we read, we bathe and dress in the course of the everyday. We will not succeed in prayer by seeming to separate the bread of the Mass from the bread of our dinner table: rather, we succeed by making all of these things with strength, simplicity and great beauty. This does not "bring down" the Mass, but proclaims that ours is a faith forever bound up with the stuff of everyday life, with incarnation.

Those who select benches and vessels and vestments and all else must look to those who know how to fashion wood and clay and glass and fabric and all with care and dignity. Seldom, if ever, will they look to those who mass produce "church goods." The local church's artists may be able to supply some of the objects to be used in the worship space and in the liturgy, but generally the parish should seek out and commission competent craftspeople and artists to create in textiles, clay, wood, glass and metal.

Like the musicians, who must not only be schooled in music but must have vital sense for liturgy, the artists must know not only what is beautiful but what is capable of serving this community's prayer. A direct application of this comes in the care these ministers have for the seasons of the liturgical year. They seek for the ways in which Lent, for example, is present in the room. What are its colors, textures, shapes, objects? Answers depend on probing the scriptures and hymns and devotions of the season, on a sense for what people's lives are like these weeks, on respect for the ways that this particular parish has "housed" Lent in the past. Further, there is need to be sensitive to the impression that is made over the weeks of the seasons, and need to make evaluations and decisions about what can become a regular part of the season so that over the years we become more and more at home in our Lent.

Both sacristans and artists need a sense for the whole room, as opposed to the sanctuary alone, as important for worship: "Suitable decoration need not and should not be confined to the altar area, since the unity of the celebration space and the active participation of the entire assembly are fundamental principles. The negative aspect of this attention invites a thorough housecleaning in which superfluities, things that have no use or are no longer in use, are removed. Both beauty and simplicity demand careful attention to each piece of furniture, each object, each decorative element, as well as the whole ensemble, so that there is no clutter, no crowding. These various objects and elements must be able to breathe and function without being smothered to excess." (*Environment and Art in Catholic Worship*, 103)

The work of the sacristans of a parish ideally means more than weekly and monthly cleaning. A sacristan is needed before the weekend Masses in a parish, and between the Masses. Care for the condition of the whole room where liturgy is celebrated, as well as for the vestments, vessels, candles, bread and wine for each celebration of the eucharist, is best done by some one person or by sharing among several persons. This can relieve the presider and other ministers in the crucial moments before and after the liturgy.

Reflections

The sacristans are the homemakers of your parish, of the house of the church. List three or four qualities you would desire in a home-maker.

Very frequently there are good artists and craftspeople in our parishes or in the larger community, but because we've been so satisified with mass produced "church goods," many of the finest artists and craftspeople have been led to believe that their gifts are not needed.

How can you better use these talented people in your parish?

1. How much are the sacristans a part of your whole liturgy picture?
2. What kind of qualifications should a sacristan have?
3. What commissions has your parish given recently to artists or craftspeople and how were these persons chosen?

Other Ministers

In a ritual such as the parish Sunday eucharist or the celebration of a wedding many gifts are shared. Most of these ministries we have discussed. Some others, no less important, are mentioned briefly here.

Bread bakers. "The nature of the sign demands that the material for the eucharistic celebration appear as actual food. The eucharistic bread, even though unleavened, should therefore be made in such a way that the priest can break it and distribute the parts to at least some of the faithful." (*General Instruction*, 283) To carry out this norm—because it makes such good common sense—a parish will see that "the work of human hands" is something local, a ministry intimately bound up with the eucharist.

Movement and gesture. There is need for those with a sensitivity to movement to help all the ministries. The assembly, the presider, the lector, the acolytes and so on: all of them move in doing their parts in the prayer, all of them have occasions to use gesture. Yet few are aware of the power of movement and gesture when done well, or the power they have to dull and distract when done poorly. Ministers need the skills to make their movements and their gestures a full part of the liturgy. This is not a matter of learning to walk or to genuflect the way somebody else walks or genuflects: rather it is for the artist here to let each person find his or her own strongest expression in these gestures.

Planners and coordinators. This is the ministry commonly exercised by the liturgy committee or team. More and more, the planning is coming to mean work with the seasons of the liturgical year and with the Sundays of Ordinary Time. It will also mean planning for the various sacramental celebrations (communal penance services, confirmation, weddings). However, some of these sacramental celebrations may be seen as fitting in more and more to the seasons (communal anointing of the sick during the Eastertime, for example), and others may become the responsibility of special groups whose ministry is to work with the persons involved in a wedding, a funeral, a baptism. Apart from planning, there is the ongoing work of coordinating which means establishing some structures to see to the recruiting, training and scheduling of all the ministers. Ideally, each ministry will care for its own recruiting and training, as well as for opportunities for reflection, prayer and socializing together.

Coordination. In large parishes it is often helpful to have someone who is present before the Sunday Masses simply to make sure that the assigned ministers are present, that they come together for a few moments of prayer, that each knows any special planning that will touch on that Sunday's liturgy. This is an especially important ministry when there are to be baptisms, first communions, the use of audio-visual materials, dramatic presentation of one of the scriptures, etc.

Today many parishes have hired or are considering hiring a parish liturgy director. This person's job is not to replace any of the ministries, but to care for all of them and to give the time, creativity and imagination that will enable all the parish to pray the liturgy and to make it their own through the years.

Reflections

After instituting a variety of ministries in the parish, and making creative plans for worship, there is still the task of bringing it all together. Who will instruct the ministers about the liturgy of the season or the feast? Who takes responsibility for the coordination? Sometimes the best of plans can fail because there is no one to orchestrate the effort.

Resources for *Who Does the Liturgy?*

Certain, Stephanie, and Meyer, Marty. *Goal Setting for Liturgy Committees.* Chicago: Liturgy Training Publications, 1981.

A workbook for those whose ministry is the coordination of parish liturgy.

Fulfilled in Your Hearing: The Homily in the Sunday Assembly. (Bishops' Committee on Priestly Life and Ministry.) Washington: USCC, 1982.

A brief and very helpful description of the role and preparation of the homily.

Funk, Virgil and Huck, Gabe, eds. *Pastoral Music in Practice.* Washington: National Association of Pastoral Musicians, 1981.

A collection of articles dealing with the music ministries.

Hovda, Robert. *Strong, Loving and Wise.* Washington: The Liturgical Conference, 1976. (Now published by The Liturgical Press, Collegeville MN.)

The principles and practice of presiding: the presider's spirit, role in planning, preparation, presence, style.

Lonergan, Ray. *A Well-Trained Tongue: A Workbook for Lectors.* Chicago: Liturgy Training Publications, 1983.

The role and spirit of the lector: brief discussions and extended exercises for beginning and advanced lectors.

Series on ministries: communion, ushers, lectors, servers and musicians. Collegeville: The Liturgical Press.

Small booklets for each of these ministries describe the role and preparation of the minister.

The Mass

We discuss the Mass here in some detail because it is the most familiar of our rituals. The approach here is to the Mass as ritual. That is, of course, an incomplete way to understand the Mass. Liturgy planners and ministers, as much as, if not more than other Catholics, need to be mindful of those other dimensions: the theology and the spirituality of the Mass that give us images of the place it occupies in the life of the church and of the individual. We need to be familiar with the ways in which covenant renewal, transformation in Christ, and affirmation of our ecclesial identity are ways to talk about what the Mass is. Yet these alone are not enough when we seek to make parish Sunday Mass the ritual prayer of all the assembly week after week. For that, it is necessary to have a grasp of how the Mass is a ritual, and of how the good use of that ritual is vital to us.

Eucharist on Sunday

Much of what has been said of ritual, of the elements of common prayer, and of ministries comes together in considering the Sunday eucharist. The next pages will look at the elements of this one liturgy. Later we will see something of the liturgies of the sacraments and other occasions.

The Mass brings together two rituals which once existed separately: a liturgy of the word, and a liturgy of the eucharist. Each is influenced by its association with the other. In addition, various rites are used to help us with transitions: as we move from our various homes and individual lives into this time of prayer together (preparation rites); as we move from word to eucharist (preparation of the gifts); finally, as we move from the prayer toward home (concluding rites). All of this is quite natural: people seeking familiar ways to gather and go about their prayer.

From their very early times, Christians have gathered "to break bread" on the first day of the week, Sunday, or "the Lord's day" as they came to call it. The day after the Jewish Sabbath day, the seventh and last day of the week, was associated with "the eighth day," the day beyond time, the day of salvation. Marking this day kept the familiar rhythm of the seven day week. Christians assembled to give thanks and praise and share the holy communion. When Christians gathered on other days of the week, in their households or with larger groups, it would be to read scripture, to pray and to sing hymns, but not for eucharist.

In the course of the centuries, many things altered this practice. Very early, rites of word and eucharist were joined. In stages, the celebration of word and eucharist together, our "Mass," spread to the weekdays. Also in stages, the Mass as the action of the assembly gave way to the Mass as the ceremonial of the presider, and it made little difference whether people were present or how they participated. The Protestant reformers, for the most part, did away with the practice of Mass on weekdays, and some of their followers went even further and had eucharist on Sunday only a few times a year.

Through all of this and much more, most churches retained the association of the eucharist with Sunday. Sometimes this has been weak, and sometimes it has been maintained only through the sense of the "Sunday obligation," but it is part of our tradition that won't go away. If anything, recent practice and teaching have pointed toward enriching the weekdays, at home and in the parish, with morning and evening prayer, and so strengthening the tie between Sunday and the community's celebration of eucharist.

The first day of the week, Sunday, and the gathering for the breaking of the bread belong together. Each enhances the other. The day, kept in some way as sign of the new creation and of the freedom from death and sin, calls for eucharist. Eucharist, as proclamation of the death and resurrection of the Lord until he comes, needs a Sunday, the day of the Lord kept holy by the people. That means something more than trying to work Mass into a busy schedule. It means that Sunday makes way: it sets us free from the million cares, free to pray over them, free to listen to the scriptures, free to remember and celebrate what may get lost in the week. We are human. We are active but need contemplation too. We need the rhythms of the one day set off against the other six.

In the end, everything has to work together: individual and family efforts to make Sunday special and to lead up to and away from the Mass, and the efforts of liturgy planners and ministers to do liturgy so well that all present will know they do the eucharist together.

Reflections

Sunday—a day of liberation, a day of space, a time of memory, a time for recreation, a space to gather, a place for gathering, a gathering for worship in thankfulness.

Do you anticipate Sunday? Do you gather yourself, your family, your community on this day? What does Sunday feel like? What would you like it to feel like?

Eucharist on Sunday will demand not only a serious, thorough planning of the liturgy, but a continuing effort to renew the importance of Sunday as the Lord's day. Good Sunday worship demands that Christians begin to make the Lord's day something different in their lives.

1. We may criticize people who look at Sunday Mass simply as an obligation, but do we support that attitude in the way we care for the liturgy?

2. How is Sunday Mass celebrated differently than weekday Mass?

Gathering

We are not like television sets, able to flip from one channel to another in seconds. We need ways to pass more slowly from one time to the next. Sometimes the way we construct spaces helps this: we have lobbies, entrance ways, yards, waiting rooms, and other assorted "in-between" spaces. We do the same with our time: the small talk that often needs to come before the business at hand, the whole system we have for leading up to saying goodbye. We help each other in and out of moments together.

People who meet to pray are no different. The rites that come before we begin the scripture readings at Mass are introductions of one sort or another, preliminaries, ways to ease into this activity. But even before we come to the entrance hymn, or the sign of the cross together, we have the less formal rituals of gathering: all that happens from the time we walk toward the church until the first hymn.

These informal moments can be crucial. It is here that the ushers are so important as greeters, hosts, ministers of hospitality. It is here that all must be in readiness for the liturgy, without last minute dashing around by any of the ministers. The whole atmosphere must be one of welcoming, open to those who would like to sit or kneel quietly and to those who might exchange greetings with friends. Sometimes there will be music for all to practice, sometimes instrumentalists might provide music as people gather. Lighting can also be important (here and throughout the liturgy) in the atmosphere that it sets and in the emphasis that it lends. The informal moments end when the word of welcome is spoken by song leader, cantor, usher or commentator. Then we may all be asked to stand and sing. This is not a song "to welcome our celebrant." The singing is to "deepen the unity of the people, and introduce them to the mystery of the season or feast" (*General Instruction*, 25).

"The parts preceding the liturgy of the word, namely, the entrances, greeting, penitential rite, Kyrie, Gloria, and opening prayer or collect, have the character of introduction and preparation. The purpose of these rites is to help the assembled people make themselves a worshiping community and to prepare them for listening to God's word and celebrating the eucharist." (*General Instruction*, 24)

This note on the character of these rites is extremely important. They must first be seen for that which they intend: introduction, preparation, helping people make themselves a worshiping community. If this is so, then the parts of the entrance rite cannot be just so many units to be run through one after the other. They must somehow happen so that their purpose is achieved: namely, at the end of the entrance rites, when we sit to hear the scriptures, we should feel like a community and we should have picked up something of the mood for today's liturgy of the word. Note that it is something of the *mood* that we receive, not a summary of what is to come through the stating of "themes."

The *Directory for Masses with Children* recognizes that our introductory rites are too crowded with small pieces that do not do their work well. "It is sometimes proper to omit one or other element of the introductory rites or perhaps to enlarge one of the elements. There should always be at least some introductory element, which is completed by the opening prayer or collect." (40) Perhaps the direction set here may be more widely applied in the future. Balance, a good flow, and timing are qualities to look for. The whole introductory rite is to be just that: an introduction. Introductions, though, too easily grow to be events in themselves.

Singing together, good processional instrumental music, a beautiful procession through the assembly, a strong greeting and the sign of the cross as a common gesture, these and the silence leading to the prayer have potential for building a sense of being *together* at prayer. Even so, they can take on different character and emphasis with the seasons. Pace is extremely important.

The penitential rite is a difficult part of the entrance rites. It is a litany of praise for God's loving kindness to us. While this is certainly one way of getting together to pray, it is difficult to achieve when wedged between so many other ways. The same is true of the Gloria (a piece to be sung unless the assembly can recite it with great energy).

Reflections

Those few minutes before Mass begins are precious moments to prepare ministers and assembly for worship.

For the ministers in a liturgy, the time before Mass should be a final check of responsibilities, but it should also get beyond that and be a quiet time: perhaps a brief moment of prayer together.

The assembly may need to be prepared with music rehearsal or some short introduction to the liturgy of the day. If so, there should usually be some silent time or reflective prelude offered before the procession begins.

1. How is the time before a Mass used in your parish?
2. How would you describe the mood in the church right before Mass begins? Commotion? Anxious anticipation? Peacefulness? Coldness?
3. Latecomers to Mass: do you think of this as just a little problem that will never go away, or does it seem like a real obstacle to good liturgy which must be solved?

The Liturgy of the Word: 1

The way Christians tell their story in ritual owes much to the ritual storytelling of the Jewish communities at the time of Jesus. The central aspect of this was and is the reading of the scriptures. These are the writings that have the narratives, poetry, prophecy, laws and letters that go to make up our story. The liturgy of the word is simply a structure to allow the reading and the listening to be done effectively, beautifully, and in common.

The pattern that has come down to us calls for two or three readings from the scriptures, with the last one taken from the gospels. What surrounds this assists the listening and the reflecting on what is heard. There is an overall flow to this rite: scripture, silence, psalm, scripture, silence. Then the gospel, surrounded with acclamation and the homily. The rite concludes with the prayers of intercession. Without care, though, the entire rite becomes one little group of words added to another. The rhythm of this rite is in the flow back and forth of word, silence, music. Each element must be presented and must be done well. And then all depends on their relationship: on the pace that puts everything together and gives a sense for the whole.

Our church has attached much importance to the basic ritual of reading and listening. Whether we gather for eucharist or for baptism or for another rite, the church's book is opened and read. In the present arrangement of the scriptures (that is what the lectionary is), the Sundays of Ordinary Time have a continuous reading through the New Testament letters (in the second reading) and through the gospels: Matthew in Year A, Mark in Year B, Luke in Year C. During the special seasons of the year, this continuous reading is broken as we turn to those passages which are the very foundation of Advent and Christmastime, Lent and Eastertime.

It is the task of lectors, deacons and priests to read the scriptures so that they command the attention of all. It is the task of the assembly to listen. Reading along with the lector is not listening. We gain far more if we fix our gaze on the reader and cling to every word.

Through the year-in, year-out and listening to our scriptures, we are formed, challenged, comforted and embraced by God's word. The homilist—facing the Sunday's readings in the context of the readings of the whole season or the continuous reading of Ordinary Time—is to make certain that the word and community confront each other.

The churches have attached much importance to the continuous telling of the story, year in and year out, through centuries. The scriptures for the coming Sunday should be readily available for reading, reflection and discussion by individuals and families as preparation for coming to the liturgy. Planners and homilists need a sense for the way the scriptures are used through the three cycles of the lectionary. They need to be aware, for example, of "Year A" as the "Year of Matthew," of the way the scriptures of each seasons (Advent, Christmastime, Lent, Eastertime) have their own integrity, of the flow of the continuous reading of Paul's letters and of the gospels through the Sundays of ordinary time.

It is generally destructive to isolate one Sunday from another by seeking in each one some "theme." Instead, planners look at the overall spirit or mood of the various liturgical seasons, and read each Sunday's scriptures in that spirit. During ordinary time, planners need some feeling for just that: the ordinary, the way the story continues from week to week.

It is not, then, a matter of saying: The scriptures today are about justice, therefore let us find songs about justice, a homily about justice, banners about justice and so on. It is rather to have some feeling that these scriptures, which are about many things on many levels, justice being one of them, are—if well told—but one expression and experience of an Advent or of the course of the story in August. The telling of the story in this rite is never intended to take out all the poetry, to say "it means just this or just that." We stick with the scriptures, and not books of theology or lives of saints, precisely because they open up, rather than limit and define. They are not historical data or somebody else's piety. They are free to be about me, about anyone, about us. They can be my story, our story, when as the church we hear and reflect.

Reflections

The way we celebrate the liturgy of the word can often betray our poor understanding of the books we use in ritual. Somehow or other we can't seem to break out of the habit of moving nonstop from one text to the next, as if that's all it would take for good worship, never leaving room for silence, reflection, or the pacing of the elements together. Neither the lectionary nor the sacramentary are automatic ritual formulas. They are there to be listened to, responded to, not just mechanically read through.

Demonstrate two different styles for the liturgy of the word. In one style, move from one text to the next without music or time for silence. In the next demonstration, use two readers and move slowly from one text to the next, using music for a response to the first reading after a period of silence.

What do missalettes do to the rhythm and flow of the liturgy of the word?

The Liturgy of the Word: 2

In this section and the next we will look at each of the moments in the ordinary structure of the liturgy of the word.

The first reading. Ordinarily, the Sunday liturgy has two scriptures before the gospel. The first of these will usually be from the Hebrew Scriptures and will ordinarily have some relation with the day's gospel. This relationship is not one of opposition, of the "old" and the "new," of the "partial" and the "complete," the "shadow" and the "reality." Rather, it is one of continuity "of our faith with the earlier covenant." (This is the emphasis in the 1975 Vatican guidelines for Jewish-Catholic relations.) The use of the Hebrew Scriptures in our Sunday liturgies says clearly that our faith did not originate in Jesus, that in fact we will only understand Jesus and his preaching and deeds when we are immersed in the whole of the scriptures which we call holy, especially those which formed Jesus himself. So often introductory comments to this scripture give the impression that it is somehow only setting us up for the real thing. That is not true. In care of preparation, in attention from the assembly, the first reading is as important as those that follow. How it is handled may well determine whether the readings that follow are listened to.

Silence. The *General Instruction* notes that there are many times when silence is to be part of the ritual. Among these is a silence after each of the first two readings and a silence after the homily. It is needed when the scripture has been done well: there's something to reflect on, an appreciation for a quiet moment to turn it over, or to let one word or phrase echo back and forth in one's mind. It is silence *together*—for all the ministers and others in the assembly. No one is busy getting music or book or papers ready (or seating latecomers). When the length of the silence is the same week after week, there is no nervous wondering when it will end. It must be a habit.

Responsorial psalm. The responsorial psalm grows out of the silence. It does not come as a sharp break. It is not a time to have a book in hand. The psalm simply flows from the silence, without announcement or disturbance. It continues the reflection. This is why it is suggested that a single refrain be used for each of the liturgical seasons and several for ordinary time: in word and in melody these pick up the mood of the time, tying the weeks together. This also frees the assembly from the printed page for better reflection and response. These seasonal psalms and refrains will be found in the lectionary. The rhythm of the liturgy of the word makes it obvious that singing is needed here, not another set of spoken words.

Second reading. Here we read from the letters of Paul and others. During the seasons these are specially selected. During ordinary time we have a continuous reading from the letters, week by week, that makes no effort to relate this text to the first reading or to the gospel: it is simply a progression through the epistles. This can call for extra efforts in preparation by the reader, especially when it is helpful to make a connection between this reading and the selection read the week before. The fact that this second reading follows its own path through one portion of scripture also suggests that a different lector read it, making it all the more obvious that we do not have a unifying theme to the elements from the story that are read, but find ourselves at different places in the gradual movement through the whole of the scriptures. We do not need a common theme to "unite" the three readings. Even on an intellectual level we are capable of keeping separate strands going at the same time. We do this with comic strips, soap operas, developing stories from the front pages.

Silence. Again, a period for silence, and stillness, follows the reading. It is needed not only for reflection, but to allow the acclamation and gospel to be strong. The contrast is very important.

The Liturgy of the Word: 3

Acclamation. "The acclamations are shouts of joy which arise from the whole assembly as forceful and meaningful assents to God's word and action. They are important because they make some of the most significant moments of the Mass (gospel, eucharistic prayer, Lord's Prayer) stand out. It is of their nature that they should be rhythmically strong, melodically appealing, and affirmative. The people should know the acclamations by heart in order to sing them spontaneously." (*Music in Catholic Worship*, 53) The *General Instruction* reinforces this by noting that when the alleluia is not sung, it may be omitted: you can't make an acclamation without raising the voice in some way, either shouting or singing. So here the alleluia, or other acclamation during Lent, breaks the silence with sound and with movement. The acclamation is really not only the singing, it is also the solemn procession with the book of the gospels, accompanied by candles or by incense, to the ambo. It is the standing up of the assembly and all the ministers. It is a needed moment after the listening and reflection. With just a brief introduction from the organ, or sung introduction from the cantor, everyone should be able to take up the alleluia.

Gospel. The reading of the gospel begins with the greeting from the presider or deacon and the solemn announcement and response, along with the customary sign of the cross on forehead, lips and heart. At its conclusion, there is a special response, and the one who has read may kiss the book. Candles and incense to honor the gospel may add to this moment. All such elements make it crucial that these most familiar stories of all be given every effort by the reader so their power can be felt.

Homily. The presider or deacon has the task of sharing reflections on the day's scriptures. It is not a time out but is as much a part of our liturgy together as anything else. The ways in which the story is truly *ours* are opened up here. The homily is a kind of dialogue with the story, the scriptures of the day. Attention is demanded of the assembly, hard work in preparation and delivery from the homilist.

Silence. Again when the homilist is seated, there are some moments of silence and stillness for reflection.

Creed. On Sundays and great feasts, the creed is recited after the homily. Sometimes this is presented as an opportunity to respond to readings and homily with an affirmation of faith. In fact, however, it is very difficult to make such a long formula feel like an affirmation. It often comes across as an interruption when the other parts of the liturgy of the word have been done well.

General intercessions. The prayer which concludes the liturgy of the word is an ancient way of praying, a litany, whose context is equally ancient and very human: intercession, placing our condition before our God. This prayer comes at what seems a "right" moment: the listening and reflecting are finished, the church has been gathered by God's word, and people have been quiet, except for brief acclamations, for some time now. A very involving prayer is needed, and that is what the general intercessions intend. There is the briefest invitation from the presider, then the litany of petitions begins. Litanies are best sung rather than recited because they depend so much on the strength of the repetition. More than the same words coming over and over again, we need the same *sounds* and flow that music can give (as when the litany of the saints or of the Blessed Virgin is chanted with the strong "Ora pro nobis"—"Pray for us"—coming again and again and again). In the intercessions, the assembly is asked to pray for the church, for authorities, for all the oppressed, for the local community. It needs to be strong in its rhythm, giving support to the feeling of a community at prayer, a community directed to the service of the world. It is the prayer of the church and should feel and sound like it. At the end, the presider draws the prayer to a brief conclusion.

Reflections

The acclamation can be enhanced when the motion of standing up is completed with a gesture of praise, as when all lift their arms together at a given moment in the singing.

In some places it has become customary to repeat the alleluia after the gospel and thus to surround the reading with acclamation.

1. What adaptations could be made for the liturgy of the word when large numbers of children are present?
2. How can a congregation appreciate silence?
3. How can the general intercessions best be prepared and prayed?
4. How attractive is the parish's book of scriptures?

The Preparation of the Gifts

Following the intercessions and before the eucharistic prayer there come some rather informal moments, moments that are more private and relaxed. Like the opening rites, this is a time of transition. The preparation of the table for the eucharist and the collection are the only "tasks" of this rite.

The bread and wine are not brought forward with great ceremony. It is setting the table. To have some people from the assembly assist in this says well whose table it is, and who provides the bread and wine. It is not the best place for songs about offering, or for any singing at all by the assembly. There might be instrumental or choral music which would support the mood of these moments.

The acolytes, deacon and presider prepare the table. The only things placed on the table, other than the altarcloth, are the vessels with the bread and wine and the book. A single container holds enough bread for everyone present; the directives are very clear in stating that the bread should be consecrated at the Mass, not taken from the tabernacle. This vessel should correspond to the kind of container we would expect to hold bread. For the wine there is a chalice and a glass flagon or other vessel which can hold a quantity sufficient to share with all present. The vessels should make their task obvious: to hold *bread*, to hold *wine*. For the book: if some support is needed, a stand or cushion, this should not be so large as to be distracting. We should avoid large microphones and other distractions on the table.

When other objects are brought forward as part of the preparation rite, the bread and wine will not be the focal point. Anything which is part of the feast or season could be present from the beginning of the liturgy or would be carried in the entrance procession. This part of the Mass is a preparation of the gifts and table for the eucharist.

Lack of pomp does not mean that there is nothing special surrounding the preparation of the table, but that this should be found in simple and reverent handling of the vessels containing the bread and wine. The bread, which is unleavened but must be seen (and touched, tasted, smelled) as "actual food" (*General Instruction*, 283), and the wine themselves inspire this reverence: God's gifts and the work of human hands. Some have expressed fears that if the bread of the eucharist does not seem entirely different from everyday forms of bread, people will cease to hold it in reverence. But the point we Christians make at eucharist is that it is precisely in the ordinariness of everyday bread, of food and of communion together, that we meet the Lord. We are to be a people who regard every bit of bread and every person who shares it with reverence. At Mass, the reverence with which the bread and wine are handled may extend to honoring them with incense.

The *General Instruction* notes that this "is also the appropriate time for the collection of money or gifts for the poor and the church. These are to be placed in a suitable area, but not on the altar" (49). The order given—the poor, then the church—may be surprising, but certainly reflects the faith of those who have come together to do the eucharist. The collecting of the money is the duty of the ushers. Their manner reflects their basic task of hospitality. Enough people should be involved so that the time give to this is not out of proportion to other parts of the liturgy. All the members of the assembly should take part in this sharing, including those involved in special ministries.

The preparation time concludes with the presider asking all to pray together about the action we are now to begin. It seems fitting that the assembly remain seated until all have answered "Amen" to the prayer over the gifts which concludes this time of preparation, but the custom of standing before the prayer over the gifts has a firm hold in most places.

Reflections

To ready ourselves for any proper meal we need space and time. How do you prepare for a family meal? What are the essentials?

While we want to avoid pomp in bringing the gifts to the table, we also want to avoid sloppiness or a casualness that turns the preparation of gifts into a relocation of bread and wine from the back of the room to the altar. An usher or liturgical coordinator can appoint people before Mass to carry the gifts to the table so that there is no rush to find gift bearers at the last minute. An usher or coordinator can instruct the gift bearers before Mass in how to hold the vessels, how to walk in procession to the table and how to return to their places in the assembly.

The Liturgy of the Eucharist: The Eucharistic Prayer

The second ritual part of the Mass is the eucharist itself: the blessing over the bread and wine, the breaking of the bread, the holy communion. These three moments together we know as eucharist, and eucharist for Christians has been a way to grasp what our lives are all about. Eucharist is the praise of God, it is being thank-filled, a way of life rather than an occasional "thank you." True to our roots in Judaism, when this way of living and being is expressed in a word, in a rite, it is to bless God, to praise God, over one another, over creation, over events. The rite with which Christians have most identified themselves from their very early years was such a blessing, the praise and thanks given to God over the bread and cup, a rite familiar from the daily and the festival prayer of observant Jews and filled with associations with Jesus.

There are a number of problems with the way we generally encounter the eucharistic prayer today. In form, it comes across as a monologue containing the story of the last supper, a monologue occasionally interrupted for a bit of reciting or singing by the assembly. We have little sense for gathering around the holy table where bread and wine—by their beauty and presence—evoke memories of Jesus and of all God's love for us, evoke wonder and thanks. A more serious problem is that the constant giving of praise and thanks does not fill our days and so we have little to bring to this kind of moment. Where do we learn to give the kind of thanks that our faith is about?

At this point in the renewal of liturgical prayer, we can only begin to acquire some sense of what this ritual is to feel like. This prayer must be the praise and thanks of God by the whole assembly: it is worded by the presider, but in the acclamations there comes a sense for this as the prayer and doing of the whole church present. The second eucharistic prayer for Masses with children has shown very clearly how acclamations—whether occuring often as they do here or limited to the Holy, memorial acclamation and Amen—are crucial to the experience of the eucharistic prayer as the "center of the entire celebration." In that model, there are five acclamations before the institution narrative (when the Last Supper is recalled), two within, and five after. What has been said of posture (in *Environment and Art in Catholic Worship*) and of music and gesture (in that document and in the *Directory for Masses with Children*) indicates not only that those present are standing for this prayer, but that the acclamations are sung by heart and with enthusiasm. It is also possible that in some settings simple gestures can accompany this singing and give an added dimension to total participation in the great thanksgiving prayer.

The role of the presider is crucial. He is to invite the assembly to prayer: "Lift up your hearts. Let us give thanks to the Lord." With word, posture, gesture, the presider is to make the praise and thanksgiving seen and heard, and so to invite and partake in the acclamations. The assembly does these acclamations not as little songs that happen to be placed here and there, but as joyous, ritual affirmations of what is taking place. Over the simple gifts of bread and wine, all, presider and assembly, remember Jesus and all the wonder of creation and liberation. With many different emotions, we remember and we give thanks. In its simplicity, the praise and thanksgiving can contain everything. But often the rite is treated as only a number of prayers to be said, people are left to follow along in booklets and to read "acclamations." Patterns of posture and speech make it seem that adoration and being spectators are the people's part. We have much to learn about this central prayer in our liturgy and how to experience it.

There are nine eucharistic prayers now in use in the United States. Among them they give some sense for what may vary and what is fairly consistent in the wording and shaping of this rite. And together also they give that sense that what is being done may be worded in a number of ways, but always the words are to help express the praise and thanks to God that has brought people here.

Reflections

The goal is a way of doing the eucharistic prayer that makes it an expression of praise and thanksgiving for all—week after week.

1. What in your experience has made for a prayerful rendering of the eucharistic prayer?
2. Some people hesitate to suggest a sung eucharistic prayer because, they argue, it will take too much time. Experiment by timing a carefully read eucharistic prayer and one that is sung.
3. Is there any way to assure the use of all the approved eucharistic prayers through the course of the year?

The Liturgy of the Eucharist: The Breaking of the Bread

After the great Amen, there is a change of tone. The eucharistic prayer, which has a unity from the preface dialogue to the Amen, is over. Now there are a number of brief rites which surround the eating of the bread and drinking from the cup: the Lord's Prayer, the peace, the breaking of the bread. A pause (during which the ministers of communion might join the presider at the altar) can separate the Amen from the Lord's Prayer. It is a chance to take a deep breath.

The *General Instruction* notes the tradition for using the Lord's Prayer here in the liturgy: "This is a petition both for daily food, which is provided for Christians especially in the body of Christ, and for forgiveness from sin, so that what is holy may be given to those who are prepared" (56). The Our Father has familiar words and is for everyone. Singing it may strengthen the bond that is sensed in this prayer as long as everyone present feels confident in the singing. Sometimes another appropriate sign can be the joining of hands, done simply by presider and ministers as an invitation to all present. "The entire communion rite is one of peace, solidarity, unity. These virtues and sentiments indicate the special emphasis of the communion rite and the theme that should be dominant in this part of the service. So the prayer of Jesus, at its beginning, with its articulation of our common sisterhood and brotherhood before God and our willingness to forgive one another, invites a vivid expression of oneness." (*It Is Your Own Mystery*)

There is little left of the initial resistance with which some reacted to the peace greeting. It is an ancient gesture among Christians, some mode of physical embrace within the liturgy. The peace greeting is not a time for the liturgy to turn into a social occasion, visiting and exchanging news. The greeting is a ritual, and it should be strong enough in its physical expression to convey a deep and honest sense of our bonds as church. Ushers make sure that any strangers are offered the peace of the community. All in all, the peace greeting makes a little more tangible our vision of the reign of God: "We don't have to go to church to embrace, but the church embrace is one of total, intentional and sacred mystery. Our eyes are opened to the depths of personal being—a situation in which obvious behavior, good or bad, no longer dominates our response to that person." (*It Is Your Own Mystery*)

The next moment in the rite is intimately bound to the peace which goes before and to the communion which follows. It is the breaking of the bread, the rite which, for the early church, named the whole ritual: they met for "the breaking of the bread." Who can say what the breaking of the bread means? There is something visible, bread being pulled apart, broken. This breaking, done without words, came from the family table and the meals of friends. It somehow expressed how Christians understood themselves. The gesture never disappeared, even during the centuries when communion was likely to be taken only by the priest. Today the *General Instruction* insists on bread which can be broken and distributed.

At this time additional plates and cups are brought to the table. Until now, there should have been but a single plate or basket, a single cup and one large container for wine. Now the bread is broken or distributed into the smaller plates, the wine is poured into the participation cups. Note that only when there has been some miscalculation in planning for the amount of bread needed should anyone take previously consecrated bread from the tabernacle. Using consecrated bread from the tabernacle is strongly discouraged in the *General Instruction* (56).

The full strength of our symbols is in offering the cup to all who come forward. This is fruit of the vine and work of human hands, a human expression of delight, festivity and communion. In the eucharistic liturgy, the sharing of the cup carries all of this to a far richer meaning in our sharing in the covenant. This should become the normal manner of parish eucharist.

The preparation for communion happens with a directness but with great reverence and respect for the consecrated bread and wine and for the assembly. The deacon and ministers of communion assist the presider in preparing the plates and cups. During this time, the cantor leads the assembly in another litany, the Lamb of God. The refrain "Have mercy on us" is to be used over and over again until the communion plates and cups are prepared, then the final response is sung: "Grant us peace."

Nothing at present stands in the way of the full opening up of the symbols in the eucharistic prayer, the peace, the breaking of the bread.

Reflections

We ought to pay more attention to how we celebrate this simple but powerful rite. We can begin by using more substantial portions of bread. Larger altar breads are now being made available through convents and commercial sources. Simple recipes are also readily available for parishioners who would be willing to assume responsibility for baking the unleavened eucharistic bread. The amount of bread to be used for a particular liturgy is easily judged through experience. The same is true for the wine as the cup comes to be shared at Sunday as well as weekday celebrations of the eucharist.

Discuss the ways in which the cup can be offered without undue delay in the liturgy. How many ministers of communion will be needed?

The Liturgy of the Eucharist: Communion

Immediately after the breaking of the bread, the presider invites the assembly to share in holy communion. This invitation may be worded in the customary way, or may incorporate other words from scripture or tradition. But the invitation must be beyond the words: in the tone of voice, the eyes, the posture and gesture. This is why the presider will hold out the plate and the cup as he speaks. And once the invitation is given, the communion begins. There should be no great division here, either in time or in the manner of communion, between the presider's communion, that of the other ministers, and that of the assembly. Often the best arrangement will be for the ministers to receive communion after the assembly.

We have ministers to assist the presider because the eating and drinking are a "communion:" unity is what they are all about. As much as possible, we are to be at table together; a family meal or formal banquet, not a cafeteria, should be our model. As communion from the cup is restored at Sunday Mass, additional ministers are needed so that holy communion feels like eating and drinking together. Sometimes this requires some remodeling to make extra room at the convenient places in the church. The furniture, after all, is to serve the liturgy for which the church gathers.

The manner of coming forward can itself speak loudly about the sharing. It should be neither a military drill organized by the ushers, nor a random lining up organized by no one but dominated by the swiftest. If singing is used at this time to give clear expression to communion, the assembly's part should be simple antiphons, choruses, refrains: ordinarily, nothing requiring a book. Even posture may be a sign of the common sharing. The practice of communion in the hand suggests that one hand be cupped within the other to take communion. Perhaps this posture could be used throughout the procession since people seem to feel uncomfortable with folding their hands in the traditional way, and a totally casual posture seems painfully out of place.

In many places it is common now for the minister of communion to place a hand on the head of children who have not yet begun to receive communion. This simple gesture, with or without a word of greeting or blessing, speaks well of what the holy communion is about.

In presenting the bread or cup, it is essential that there be a personal moment, meeting of eyes when one says "The body of Christ" and the other affirms, "Amen." Then the bread or cup is given from one person to another. Nothing automatic or impersonal belongs in the word or gesture of either person. The entire communion rite should say clearly that the people are a "holy communion."

After the eating and drinking, the plates and cups are returned quietly to a table on one side. The altar is empty again. The washing of the vessels may be done after the liturgy so that now there can be quiet and stillness (no one moving around) for a little while. Everyone is seated. Lighting may be turned down. Music, instrumental or choral, may sometimes be used for this meditation time. A generous space of time is needed, with consistency from week to week. This silent time too is an expression of communion. Habits of prayer need to be formed.

The communion rite, and the liturgy of the eucharist, concludes with the prayer after communion. The silence leads to this, and it is simple, short prayer, more important for giving some sound to our final thanks than for any specific content.

Reflections

We have "thing-a-fied" so much in our way of living. This attitude inhabits our economic cathedrals and our temples of worship. We can even "thing-a-fy" the eucharist into bread and wine. But eucharist is not a thing. It is sharing, a breaking of bread, a sharing of the cup.

The assembly is most personally involved at liturgy in the sharing of the bread and cup. Receiving communion from the minister can be either a treasured moment of grace or a very ordinary "handing out" ceremony. The way we share the table of unity and charity may say a great deal about how we look at ourselves as a community. When the signs of eucharist are used carefully and deliberately, it will be easier for everyone to understand what this eucharist and we as church are all about.

Concluding Rites

This is again a time of transition: from the prayer together to our individual lives. When the prayer after communion is finished, there is a sense of the last moments. It is a leave-taking rite. When friends part, they have their rituals: a hug, a wave, some formula used, "Take care," "See you soon." These are comfortable ways to get through the parting, familiar ways to express ourselves. Large groups have their rituals for the same purpose: the formal voting to adjourn, or the curtain calls at the end of a theatre presentation. Such moments mix the formal and informal, and contain much of what the whole time together was about.

At the end of the Mass, the leave-taking rite usually consists of announcements, the blessing, the dismissal, a song and procession. It is important to see these together, and to see them in light of their purpose: an ending, one that leaves good feelings about what has happened here and something of an eagerness to assemble again. If the liturgy has been good prayer together, then the closing has something bittersweet about it. Hurrying through it, letting it become just one set of words after another so that annoucements and blessing and dismissals blur together, destroys the rite.

The announcements are to be brief. They are like the welcome before the liturgy began, part of the hospitality: sharing information about the community, and doing it in an informal and friendly manner. They are not best done by the presider (since he has just done the prayer after communion and will next do the blessing) but by the one who did the first words of welcome or by one who can naturally represent the day-to-day work of this church. The last annoucement is the name and location of the closing song, if there is to be one.

The blessing is the heart of the concluding rite. Many forms for this are now provided, all building toward the final "May almighty God bless you . . ." Or that form may stand by itself. There is also the gesture: outstretched hands during the three-part blessing, and bowing of heads, and the sign of the cross during the final words. The assembly responds with "Amen" to the three-part blessings when these are used. These "Amens" need to be habitual and strong, not awkward and embarrassed mumblings. The cadence of the sung or spoken blessing words can do much to bring forth a good Amen. The words of various blessings, if some of them are used consistently, may provide forms for blessings apart from the Mass: the blessing of children at night, of one another before a journey, of the sick.

The dismissal is given by the deacon, as are many of the practical instructions for the assembly throughout the liturgy. The words can vary, but should always make it easy and comfortable for people to respond together, "Thanks be to God." The strength of the words and manner of the speaker, along with a consistent and obvious conclusion, will let that final line of the assembly be loud and firm.

What follows has no set format. In most places, it is a hymn and a procession of the ministers through the assembly. That is one approach. Another would be to let the sung blessing, with a strong "Amen" response, feel like a conclusion, and then the dismissal is just that: leaving and visiting can begin at once, perhaps with some organ or other instrumental music. Or the conclusion may somehow be tied to the entrance rites (as the Gregorian chant did when the "Ite Missa est" was sung to the same melody as the "Kyrie"). This could be done especially during the seasons, and thus echo the mood set in the entrance rite: it is a mood which is to be taken home. For this, songs from the entrance rite could be repeated, or silence when appropriate, to accompany the procession of the ministers.

The ministers, especially the ushers, still have their hospitality. This may be in visiting or in a goodbye and a smile while handing out bulletins. This last impression may be remembered longest.

Reflections

Our rites have conclusions. We care about how we end, and so begin something new. Reflect on how we express this care at: wedding receptions, cemetery burials, retirement parties, school graduations, birthdays.

Does our conclusion at eucharist deserve any less care? What new beginnings does this usher in?

When are the annoucements done—within the communion rite (before the prayer after communion) or as part of the conclusion where they belong? How are they done?

Can you describe how the mood changes from the time after communion to the moments of the blessing and dismissal?

Resources for *The Mass*

Bernardin, Joseph. *Our Communion, Our Peace, Our Promise.* Chicago: Liturgy Training Publications, 1984.

> *Pastoral letter on parish Sunday eucharist and the responsibility of the assembly.*

Directory for Masses with Children. (Sacred Congregation for Divine Worship.) Washington: USCC, 1974.

> *A document whose introductory sections are essential for all liturgy planners.*

General Instruction of the Roman Missal (with commentary by Ralph Keifer). Washington: National Asociation of Pastoral Musicians, 1980.

> *The 1969 Instruction (with later updates) and a commentary. This document defined the order of the Mass following the dictates of the Constitution on the Sacred Liturgy.*

Jarrell, Stephen. *Guide to the Sacramentary for Sunday and Festivals.* Chicago: Liturgy Training Publications, 1983.

> *A week-by-week discussion of the options offered in the sacramentary.*

Kay, Melissa, ed. *It Is Your Own Mystery.* Washington: The Liturgical Conference, 1979.

> *Reflections on the order of the communion rite and the ministries involved.*

Lectionary for Mass: Introduction. Washington: USCC, 1982.

> *The 1982 revision of the introduction to the lectionary is a concise but thorough understanding of the order and ministries involved in the liturgy of the word as well as the role and structure of the lectionary. A commentary on the Introduction, written by Ralph Keifer, is published by the National Association of Pastoral Musicians.*

Searle, Mark. *Liturgy Made Simple.* Collegeville: The Liturgical Press, 1981.

> *An outstanding introduction to the structure and celebration of Sunday Mass.*

Seasoltz, Kevin, ed. *Living Bread, Saving Cup: Readings on the Eucharist.* Collegeville: The Liturgical Press, 1982.

> *Articles previously published in* Worship *on a variety of questions related to the eucharist.*

Days and Seasons

The seasons and festivals of the church year are basic to planning liturgy, and to the way home and parish together shape prayer and lives. These brief introductions try only to suggest something of the mood or spirit that each season calls from us.

Naming the Days

In all our different groups, we name the days. As citizens of the United States, we name Independence Day. As music lovers, we name Beethoven's birthday. As Irish-Americans we name Saint Patrick's Day. As a couple, we name a day our anniversary. We scatter such special days throughout the ordinary ones, giving the year a rhythm of anticipation: How many days is it until . . .? Some of our special days grow beyond their 24 hours and create a whole season: a short one like the Thanksgiving Day weekend, or a long one like the weeks before Christmas.

The days we have named are meant to be kept. We *keep* days (as in "Are you keeping Lent this year?" or "Remember to keep holy the Sabbath day") by holding to them, remembering them and letting them stir memories in us, as a wedding anniversary or Fourth of July is supposed to do. We keep them by letting the memories lead to observances, little rites of word or deed with which we mark the day: the birthday cake, the firecrackers, the Halloween costumes. We keep the days—*and the days keep us!* That happens with the wedding anniversary: we remember the day, we surround it with specialness, and it tells us who we are, keeps us who we are. Or we keep the Fourth of July with parades, song, music, gatherings outdoors, fireworks—and doing that *re-creates* us as something more like a free people. Or, in the recent past (and perhaps again now), we Catholics kept Fridays by not eating meat, and somehow our solidarity in this kept us, gave us a sense of belonging within a church, identified us to ourselves and to others.

That kind of community is basically what the naming and keeping of days and seasons is all about. They are ways that go beyond textbooks, beyond statements of creed, beyond even common convictions about morality: they gather this and all else in life into ways we can make it all very personal and yet shared. Seasons and days that we name let us take all that it is to be Christian and express it in songs, in stories, in dances, in colors and textures and much more. To do this, and do it over and over through the years, is the way a people hands on faith generation to generation. It happens only within a people, not in abstract. The stories we tell and all the other rites of the seasons are open enough, even ambiguous enough, to remain strong year after year.

And that is the point. They are my story, our stories. They are about me, my life, about us, our life together as church. And so the songs and other rites of each season: their strength is in the way they are *not* pieces of data somewhere out there which the individual is to approach, study, and perhaps adapt to. Rather, they are inside us, and the task of those who would help to create an Advent or an All Saints Day is to be in touch with what it is inside every person that is being called forth in this particular day or season. The feasts and the seasons are not gimmicks to present lives of Jesus and the saints. We need to name our days and to keep them: they are about us and what it is to be the church.

The first day we name is Sunday. This we keep with Mass together, and in other ways, to make it a "kingdom" day, a day of new creation and of freedom from slavery and sin and death. Sunday is called the "eighth" day, the day that is beyond our cycle of time. It is called the Lord's day and thus it stands first in our calendar, marking the rhythm of our lives with the proclamation of the word and the breaking of the bread.

Many Sundays come within our seasons of Advent, Christmastime, Lent and Eastertime, and here the Sunday liturgy takes on the mood and spirit of that season. These seasons are larger than their Sundays, however, and seek ways to be kept beyond the eucharist liturgy. A season has its own spirit: we seek this in words and stories that catch something of it, or in various sounds that bring it to us, or in ways of moving, or in all sorts of uses of color and materials. We never really pin that spirit down, saying "Advent means just such and such." We only deal with it in words of poetry, for it is too close to us for anything else.

The work of the liturgy is to express something of this spirit and to do so in a way that can bring the Advent or the Lent out of people, more each year, until the keeping of the seasons tells us we belong here.

Reflections

"Keeping the day"—this phrase seems to give a freedom and a belonging! What day will you name and keep within the next few months? What rituals of anticipation will you perform? Have others kept this day before you? How long is the "day"? Twenty-four hours? A week? What stories will surround the "naming"?

The keeping of holidays, feasts and seasons helps us maintain a necessary rhythm and vitality in our lives. We need these special days to lift us out of the ordinariness of everyday. Holidays, feasts and seasons are not for producing things or accomplishing great goals. They are simply days to enjoy, to remember, to be in touch with our history, our relationships, our tradition of faith. They point to a deeper and more profound sense of who we are and where we are going: not in any intellectual or academic manner, but in a way that allows our entire selves to celebrate.

1. What days are really special in your parish?
2. What do we do besides use the sacramentary's proper prayers to commemorate a feast or keep a season?
3. Think of a feast day celebration you greatly enjoyed. What made it so?

Advent

It has been common for peoples to surround the shortest, darkest and perhaps very cold days of the year with special ritual. This has often had in it something of both fear and promise. For some, that was the simple fear of the dark and cold: realities we have found ways to avoid, though we still fear them. And it was fear that the precious food supply might not last until there could be new planting and growth and harvest. The promise which ran through the beginning days of winter often took shape in the sun which at least ended its descent and began to stay just a bit longer each day, pledging better days ahead. Christians, in placing festivals for the birthday of Jesus and his manifestation around the winter solstice, were doing what came naturally. The anticipation and the celebration of those events, birth and manifestation, were our way to "talk" of what fear and promise meant in the church.

But more than just talk. The days that came to be known as Advent were never meant only to teach something about Christ's coming in past, present and future. They are expressions of an advent that is inside each of us. Part of that is the fears we have, all of them. They do not center on any one time of year, our fears, but being afraid is as much a part of the human condition now as ever, maybe even more. These are private, family, community fears. Somehow, then, what we do in Advent—the stories we tell, songs we sing, customs we observe—lets us admit to those fears. More than this, the keeping of Advent puts that fear up against a promise: not in some historical sense of foretelling the coming of Jesus who has now come, but in the sense that being the church is a response to God's promise and is somehow itself a promise to one another and to the Lord.

And that, perhaps, says a little about the feeling that these days before Christmas have. But the more effective way to enter into Advent, to begin to feel at home here, is to seek it out inside us and inside Advent's own texts and music and colors. A good beginning may be a search through the scriptures of Advent's Sundays and weekdays. What are the key words, words that open up the mood? Every list will be different, but as an example: leap, sing, be with child, bloom, stay awake, steady, await, kiss, bring forth, stand up straight, filled, made low, be strong, be opened, be cleared, burn, spring, look down, withered, vanish, sway, climb, clear, rescue, walk, look forward, overshadow.

These are strong images. How do they then express themselves? Phrases from "O come, O come, Emmanuel" or from "Wake, awake," or from the "O" antiphons? Or what do such images sound like not in church music but in popular music, or classical or folk or rock or jazz? Each type of music must sometimes be expressing the advent that is in the composer or performer. Or, what musical instruments sound like these images? Or, what stories do such images point to? Stories from scripture, yes, but also stories from the newspapers, from novels, from the movies? What characters seem to have something really like Advent about them?

If Advent has its words, its music (and other sounds too), its stories, it also has its colors (and not just purple), its textures, its designs. Do the colors blend or are they in sharp contrast during Advent? And it even has its tastes: is it sour, sweet, bitter, sweet and sour, bland, salty, rich? People may name these differently, that is natural, but there will be overlapping and building to show what a sense we may already have of this season.

Liturgy is to let that shape our prayer during these weeks. With a great simplicity so that the words may be heard, the music be felt, the colors be seen, and with much consistency from week to week, Advent comes out and takes shape in the community. Words and tunes and colors and stories are all woven together, a whole, a time we can come home to year after year.

Reflections

Search the scriptures and music of Advent and let the words rise to meet you. Make your list of strong words and phrases. Spend time in meditation and/or sharing your lists.

We Christians don't often discuss together the longings, the waitings, the darkness we feel deep within ourselves. Perhaps we judge these feelings to be uniquely our own or else just not the kind of thing we should be sharing. But they are our common ground for celebrating Advent! Ultimately, all the longing and waiting in our lives leads toward the Lord.

1. What has been the mood of Advent in your life? How does that match the parish celebration of Advent?
2. How can liturgy express the longing hearts of the people?
3. What would we lose if we eliminated Advent from our calendar?

Christmastime

One thing that is behind the heart's beat in these days is this: birth. It is the story of a birth, Christmas. More than birth, of course. Word-made-flesh, but before that you have to pause just a bit on birth itself. Before it is marvelous that there is incarnation, it is marvelous that any new person bursts forth and, the cord cut, cries a very personal cry.

Births fill our folklore. Even our ancestors, who lived closer than we to such things, never could get over what a wonderful thing it was: this event that stands between the generations, that changes most everything, that at once promises us a future and sentences us to the past. For the delight had always just a bit of the fear: the new always does that to human beings and their societies. Herod acts out the side of us that sees in every birth our own death coming closer. Perhaps the mystery and awe and song inspired by birth could not be so great without this darker side.

Stories of marvelous births fill our fairy tales, our myths, our stories from the Hebrew Scriptures; Sarah's laugh resounds through a thousand birth stories of all peoples. It may be that something-more-than-meets-the-eye element in the birth of Jesus, the incarnation then, that made December 25 just the right date. Birth, after all, is normally a thing of springtime so that the newborn can grow strong before the cold and perhaps hunger come again. But here is something else: a birth in winter, born with the weak sun.

The first thing liturgy has to do is let this story overpower us. It is a "once upon a time" story, the kind that is more true than the temperature and time of day. There is something in us that does yet thrill to hear of a birth and that is absolutely convinced that the only way things hold together is that there is God all mixed up in our clay. Only when we are thus swept off our feet will we know that the Christmas prayer that springs from this story doesn't begin in explanations or theology as such, but in all those human arts that touch the story and so open its myriad wonders.

Christmas as a season may seem a lost cause. What energy is left after the American pre-Christmas season? Yet there is still enough festivity called forth by the telling of the story of this birth, enough to take us through New Year's and to Epiphany. We compete with the world already when we decide to wait through an Advent, when we say that you can't hear the story in its awesomeness, you can't sing the Christmas songs and wear the Christmas colors and make a festival of it—unless you wait. That done, extending the festival for the season seems easy. Ordinarily there are five times of gathering during the season: Christmas itself, Holy Family, New Year's, Epiphany, the Lord's baptism. The shape of the liturgy for these days can have a certain consistency while letting scriptures and homily give each its special note.

Local traditions may say much of certain apsects of Christmas day itself: where the creche goes and how, who sings the Midnight Mass, where the flowers are placed. Hospitality may flourish for some of the Christmas Day Masses as nowhere else in the year. Anything worth so much effort is worth savoring in the days that follow. Some of the sounds can be sustained through Epiphany, some of the flowers, some of the special scents of many candles and of incense. The images evolve within this time, dwelling on one after another of the moments in the stories of birth and manifestation. In the "twelve days of Christmas" and in various ethnic customs associated with the season, with Epiphany as much as with Christmas, we sense the possibilities. The celebration is poetic, not bound to literal understandings of the sequence of events, but bounding around, mixing up, touching on what's just beyond the rational. Manger and magi and gifts of gold are all mixed up with water turned to wine and Jesus deep in the Jordan river beside John. You can't really explain what's going on here—and you don't have to.

Reflections

A start for a Christmas list of words from liturgy and culture: birth, gift, bells, light in darkness, lightheartedness, the unexpected, stars in sky and eyes, stories, manifestations. Carry it on!

There is something born again in all of us at Christmas. There is a feeling of warmth and of friendship. Christmas puts us in touch with each other and amazes us again with the remarkable story of how much a part of us our God chooses to be. There is a sense of peace and good will we hope will somehow last through the year.

1. Some parishes plan very fine celebrations for Christmas Day, but then let Holy Family, Mary, Mother of God and Epiphany slip away. How can all these days be woven together into one joyous holiday?

2. Christmas is a homecoming feast. Old parishioners, college students and infrequent worshipers come home to celebrate Christmas. How can all these homecomers be made to feel welcome?

Lent

The season of Lent developed as days of preparation for Easter and, more exactly, as days of preparation for the Easter initiation of catechumens into the fullness of the community. Over a period of time the keeping of forty days became the common practice, and the entire community went into the season with those about to be initiated and with those who were returning to the faith. Even when there were no catechumens preparing for baptism, Lent remained a season turned toward the renewal of baptism: to hear the gospel well, to take it in with great seriousness, to experience something of the dying and rising that baptized life is all about.

Lent is an intense time. It begins with stark and basic actions that continue to speak to people: the marking with ashes. Ashes, in the time of year when things are yet very bleak, are an image of what is common to all the living: the end of everything, the beginning of everything. On this Wednesday, while life bustles on, Christians are marked with ashes by ministers themselves marked with ashes. The ashes call into question all that bustling life, all our selves. There is something here about working through the pretenses and getting to the real, about facades that crumble, about what our lives will be like through these forty days. The liturgy of Ash Wednesday is the marking with the blessed ashes: the scriptures accompany this as do the psalms and other singing of the day.

The Sunday scriptures of Lent, especially those in Year A, build one on the other. In themselves, the gospel readings can be viewed together to make a "lenten gospel," a story which this season as a whole tells. As always, it is about us, it is our story, as individuals and as church. The gospels can be a beginning point in seeking the shape the liturgy takes during these weeks. What does a Lent sound like? What are the rhythms, what is the volume, what is the tempo? And what is the pace? Where is the silence? Similiar questions must be put to every other art which is used in the liturgy. How does the whole then sustain and encourage the keeping of Lent in the home and the individual's life?

More and more, Lent in the parish will be marked by the presence of the catechumens during the liturgy of the word, and by the rites which mark their election (the final step of preparation before baptism), and by the special prayers on some Sundays of Lent which witness to the nearness of that baptism. These rites indicate that the catechumens are to be present only until the time of preparation for the eucharist, then they leave (usually to gather in another place for prayer and reflection on the scriptures). This is a powerful sign of what initiation into the church will mean: joining the baptized in holy communion. The presence of a group of catechumens in the midst of the church during Lent will perhaps be the greatest help in renewing this season. Could there be better witness for the baptized to the faith they have professed? What else could state so strongly what it means to be church? The presence of those who seek full belonging can put those who do belong into a well-kept Lent.

The Sunday liturgies of Lent need a consistency in song and color and pace that tie all the six weeks together. These constants should say, without anyone having to verbalize it: "This is Lent, our Lent." That comes through in the way the whole preparation rite is handled: how it differs from ordinary time and other seasons not just in some obvious song words, but in the use of silence, in the choice of instruments for the procession music, in the length and solemnity of the penitential rite. Lent is also found in the use of an appropriate refrain for the responsorial psalm, one that can be kept all through Lent; in the special gospel acclamation; in the form of the final blessing; in the way the dismissal is handled; in the use of few and basic colors in the room and in the absence of all unnecessary furniture; in special efforts to present Lent's scriptures dramatically. When the whole has this kind of unity, and this opportunity for the rites to become familiar to everyone, then the things that are unique about each week—scripture, the scrutinies of the candidates for baptism—these have a place to do their work.

Reflections

Parishes sometimes use Lent for various forms of adult education, but the lenten sacramentary and lectionary offer us the church's avenue of spiritual direction by pushing us into the depths of the paschal mystery. We discover what it means to be baptized in Christ, to be rid of sin, to belong to the church. Anything that divides our attention only weakens a good Lent.

Lent does not rest at the altar: it fills the parish. It is in our homes and our own personal way of thinking and doing things. This takes everyone's cooperation. It presumes some communal and personal disciplines. It means we might have to let go of some things that ordinarily fill our time, so that we are free for welcoming candidates for baptism and reception into the full communion, and for renewing our own baptismal vocation.

1. Why do you suppose so many people come to church on the first day of Lent for ashes?
2. What are some of your recollections of Lents in the past? How did these experiences of Lent define the season for you? What can these memories teach us about the present?
3. What powerful disciplines of Lent can we have today?

The Triduum

The Triduum ("three days") refers to the time from the evening liturgy on Holy Thursday until the evening prayer on Easter Sunday. The sacramentary says of it: "The Easter triduum of the passion and resurrection of Christ is thus the culmination of the entire liturgical year. What Sunday is to the week, the solemnity of Easter is to the liturgical year. The Easter triduum begins with the evening Mass of the Lord's Supper, reaches its high point in the Easter vigil, and closes with evening prayer on Easter Sunday." The emphasis is on the unity of the days, on not separating the death and resurrection. From its first years, the church could never speak of or understand one without the other. Triduum is a single celebration.

This means that presentations of Holy Thursday, Good Friday and Holy Saturday in terms of reenacting Jesus' last hours, death and burial are not accurate. Rather, the liturgies of these days understand that to speak of Jesus' death is to speak of his resurrection. The Triduum is the occasion for the most crucial gestures in the initiation of new Christians: the fast, the prayer, the baptism and confirmation and eucharist. The Triduum is kept as an annual Passover for the whole community, all of those whose existence is defined by those same sacraments. The church keeps the Triduum.

The bond between the Christian sacramental experience of dying and rising with Christ and the Jewish Passover is not simply that the gospels tell us it was at the time of Passover that Jesus was executed and rose from the dead. Rather, the early Jewish followers of Jesus themselves had, from their own keeping of Passover, the notions, words, experiences to name what had happened to Jesus and to them. It was the Passover festival, understood as present reality (". . . not for our ancestors only did he do this, but for us . . ."), that made what Jesus did understandable as a present reality in the church. It was Passover as memorial and dedication to freedom that gave them a way to talk about what happened in Jesus and now in the church. And it was Passover as a "not yet," as a longing for the final liberation, that kept the church's Easter human.

The power of the Holy Thursday liturgy must be in its unique gestures which summon us to memories and hopes of what it means to die and rise in Christ. A gesture like the washing of feet can convey in its own special and strong way our calling to do that, our need to have it done to us, the little ways we die and rise in such washing and being washed. The gestures say what it means to "pass over," to be church. The evening liturgy does not need embellishment in commitment services and the like.

The keeping of the Triduum until the Vigil liturgy may be marked by a number of rites and prayers, such as the services of Good Friday, but most basic is the ritual of fasting. "On Good Friday, and if possible, also on Holy Saturday until the Easter Vigil, the Easter fast is observed everywhere." (General Norms for the Liturgical Year, 18) Note that here the norms speak of an Easter fast, not the lenten fast. It is the fast of anticipation before the great festival; it is the fast of baptized and catechumens together before the Easter sacraments. It is not a fast of repentance but a fast of excitement, a fast of reverence and preparation.

The Easter Vigil is addressed thus in the Orthodox liturgy: "The spotless Passover, the great Passover, the Passover of the faithful, the Passover which opens to us the gates of Paradise, the Passover which sanctifies all the faithful. The Passover joyful, the Passover of the Lord, the Passover all-majestic has shone forth on us! With joy let us embrace one another! O Passover, release from sorrow!" The Easter Vigil is not a mere anniversary of the resurrection, but *is* the passing over to life in Christ by those being initiated and the renewing of this life in the whole church. Nothing in the whole year knows such richness as the baptizing, confirming and eucharist that tonight climax the Triduum, Lent, and the whole long catechumenate. In the vigiling and listening to the grandest stories of our scriptures, in the chants and singing, in the lighting of the new fire, in the flowing waters of baptism, in the rich perfumes of the anointing with chrism, in the blessing and sharing of bread and cup, and most of all in the people who do these things together, are expressed the whole meaning and belief of the church.

Reflections

Why do you think the church names the fast on Good Friday and Holy Saturday the "Easter fast"?

What are the other times of your life when one act unites the space of several days?

What are your experiences and memories of Good Friday and Holy Saturday? Is Easter a part of those memories?

The Triduum, one solemn commemoration of Christ's death and rising, reaches its high point at the Easter Vigil. In baptizing on this night we see more clearly than ever that the mystery of Christ, dead and rising, is not an abstract theory but an ongoing saving event that raises up our own brothers and sisters to eternal life. The candidates for baptism and confirmation become a living gospel of Christ's victory over sin and death. As the community participates in the initiation of new members, all are invited to renew baptism.

The liturgies for the Triduum are complex. Keep a careful record of plans and materials that will be useful for next year's planning.

Eastertime

Eastertime, our earliest distinct season within Christian communities, today is hardly noticed. Even before Lent took shape, there were the 50 days of rejoicing after Easter and its baptisms. The calendar reform after Vatican II not only kept Eastertime as a distinct season, but pointed to its importance by changing the way Sundays of the season are named: from "after Easter" to "of Easter." But names do not make a festive season happen. A sense for how this season can be our own, how it comes from the heart, what it is to express of the human and Christian experience—this can begin with a look at its origins.

Both Lent and Eastertime developed around the keeping of Passover which, for Christians, became the time of celebrating the sacraments of initiation. Eastertime prolonged the rejoicing. But Passover itself, the memory and the experience of deliverance from slavery, is crucial. For the Jews, this festival was and is kept with rites which told of the exodus, told of it in such a way that there was no doubt that the saving work of God was in their ancestors' escape from slavery to freedom, and in that direction at work in the life of their people at all times. What the followers of Jesus understood of him and his teaching was intimately bound up in what Passover had always meant to them.

But there is another step to take. The Jewish festival of Passover had its own roots in the springtime festivals of farmers and shepherds, festivals that rejoiced in the end of winter and the promise of life: life from the warm earth and the rains that would grow the crops, life from the new lambs being born. The community would go on. It was a matter of life and death and for this year, it was life! That was cause to rejoice, to give thanks. The life and death tale of the Hebrews, death in slavery and life in the escape to freedom, came to be told around these spring festivals. The symbols worked together: the bread and the lamb of the farmers and shepherds now tied into the story of how the people Israel were saved and how they had to go in haste. The stories and the rites evolved and their origins were often forgotten, but the springtime and the triumph of life and freedom in God's saving work were celebrated.

So Easter tells a human story, perhaps the most basic. The world has echoed it in its fairy tales and its motion pictures. In little ways, it tells itself in each human life. As Christians, all the stories we tell of exodus and of Jesus and of the dry bones and of Abraham and Isaac and of Jonah are meant to reflect what we believe about the struggle of life and death that forever grips the world and each of us. That story, and what we as church affirm as our experience, is the making of an Eastertime.

... all the
... ole but
... ne rite
... s the Easter
... at all the liturgies of the
... everywhere! There is the sound of
... that are used only during these days, and the
strong hymns of the Eastertime. Overall, the Eastertime liturgies might be known for the feeling of peace, of gentleness: the powerful silence in which the seed sprouts, the bud swells, the tomb-become-womb is touched. This is the quiet joy that permeates all the gospels of the Easter weeks: Jesus and Mary in the garden, the upper room, the stranger cooking breakfast, the Emmaus supper, the discourse from John's gospel. Every art used in liturgy is to be at the service of this spirit, shaping a way for the church to pray in these weeks, a way which can be repeated year after year. As with each season, we need to seek ways the spirit takes on sounds, colors, textures, melodies, movements. Such an Eastertime will let us celebrate with voices and eyes and hands that are deeply Christian and that can, in the Eastertime, be completely themselves.

Reflections

For the early church, the 50 days after Easter were a period of "mystagogia." This meant a time to plunge more intensely into the Easter mysteries, drawing on the experience of these mysteries in the Easter sacraments. The church believed that only after experiencing baptism could the newly initiated really understand the mysteries. Baptism was illumination: eyes were opened. The community shared in these Eastertime gatherings with the newly initiated and all together reflected on Christ's presence within their community.

Eastertime is no less important for us than for our ancestors in faith. The Eastertime lectionary and sacramentary, seen through our own personal religious experience, are marvelous aids for getting to the heart of the season.

1. How can music carry through the 50-day unity of the Eastertime?
2. How can the celebration of marriage, ordination, confirmation, first communion, anointing of the sick, and the dedication of a church during Eastertime enhance our understanding and appreciation of these days?

Festivals and Ordinary Time

The seasons of our year are anticipations of festivals and continuations of festivals. Advent and Christmastime must go together, as must Lent and Eastertime. Christmas and Easter have long been our great festivals, drawing in their circles other great days like Epiphany, Ascension and Pentecost. In thinking of these festivals or of others, we have to be serious about the very idea of festivity, for we live in a society that can label "National Buttermilk Week" as if that would mean something to the lives of people.

Festivals are not made by just naming days: naming and keeping go together, and when we speak of those in relation to true festivity, it is asking a great deal of people. Joseph Pieper writes: "To celebrate a festival means: to live out, for some special occasion and in an uncommon manner, the universal assent to the world as a whole." (*In Tune with the World*, page 23) Festivals are without wordly purpose, they are just thanksgiving and praise: "The happiness of being created, the existential goodness of things, the participation in the life of God, the overcoming of death—all these occasions of the great traditional festivals are pure gift." (page 46)

Perhaps other ages were more ready to take such pure gifts. Certainly it seems enough for us that we be ready to take Christmas and Easter (and what surrounds them) this way, to let them take us, rather, bestow on us their gifts. For now, the calendar of the church seems to recognize that the year should not be filled with various lesser festivals which go unrecognized. Instead, we have the steady marking of "Ordinary Time" between Epiphany and Lent and again from Pentecost until Advent. Perhaps this also offers a chance to grasp our original festival, the Sunday, kept as such in the home and in the church community.

The tradition has marked certain days throughout the year, mostly during Ordinary Time, to remember and celebrate some of the saints or a mystery of the faith or a title of Mary or Jesus. Only a few of these are likely to have significance in a given community, but those few should be identified and kept in special ways. The "holy days of obligation" are, in each country, an attempt to identify several such occasions. Our keeping of Assumption, Immaculate Conception, and Mary, Mother of God (the latter two coming within the Advent/Christmastime) will celebrate the place of Mary within a parish church. Our observance of the feast of All Saints is mentioned below. Ascension has its place within the season of Eastertime and Christmas is the center of the Advent/Christmastime.

The Ordinal
three year cycle. I
The different appr
tone for the Sunda
Sunday of Ordinary
for good arrangeme
gifts of all the variou
that sustains us and allows the seasons to be so special when they come

The last weeks of Ordinary Time, the weeks of November, have a special character. On these Sundays we approach the conclusion of the gospel that is being read that year, and so are hearing passages that speak of the final things. At the same time, because it stands between the rejoicing of the harvest and the short, dark days of winter, November has been a time when people in these climates inevitably have focused on death and on the dead. Halloween, with its ghosts and masks and even its tricks, is one descendant of this. So is the feast of All Saints and the emphasis in November on prayer for the dead. Our American Thanksgiving Day also seems to fit into the spirit of this month.

Certainly November is not a season in the sense of an Advent or a Lent, but it is a time that needs to express a certain spirit: the solidarity we profess with the saints and ancestors, something that has a multitude of forms in paintings, windows, statues, relics, cemeteries, litanies, hymns and chants. And all of this hands on and helps us grow—not only in that faith of communion with our saints, but in readiness to acknowledge, with Saint Francis, that in some ways death is a sister to us, another of God's servants.

Reflections

How does the Christian proclamation of the communion of saints express itself in your parish?

What feasts of the saints are celebrated by people? What are possible directions here?

What are the liturgies and prayers and devotions of November?

Resources for *Days and Seasons*

Adam, Adolf. *The Liturgical Year.* New York: Pueblo Publishing Company, 1981.
A survey of the history and current reform of the feasts and seasons.

Cassa, Yvonne, and Sanders, Joanne. *Groundwork: Planning Liturgical Seasons.* Chicago: Liturgy Training Publications, 1982.
Workbook that describes a method for a pastoral approach to the celebration of the seasons.

Huck, Gabe. *The Three Days.* Chicago: Liturgy Training Publications, 1981.
The planning and celebration of the liturgies of Holy Thursday, Good Friday and the Easter Vigil.

Huck, Gabe, and Simcoe, Mary Ann, eds. *A Triduum Sourcebook.* Chicago: Liturgy Training Publications, 1983.
Scriptures, prayers, poems, homilies and other texts that are or have been in the past part of the paschal triduum.

Nocent, Adrian. *The Liturgical Year.* Collegeville: The Liturgical Press, 1977.
Four volumes with detailed notes on the seasons and feasts, their history, theology and celebration.

Schmemann, Alexander. *Great Lent.* Crestwood NY: St. Vladimir's Seminary Press, 1969.
An Orthodox theologian, Schmemann conveys the strength and beauty of the lenten season.

Simcoe, Mary Ann, ed. *Parish Path through Advent and Christmastime.* Chicago: Liturgy Training Publications, 1983.
Articles on the scriptures, prayers, music, gestures and environment of the winter seasons.

Simcoe, Mary Ann, ed. *Parish Path through Lent and Eastertime.* Chicago: Liturgy Training Publications, 1984.
Second edition of this book has articles on the lectionary, sacramentary, music and environment of these seasons.

Other Rites

Liturgy is woven through our lives. It brings the individual and the Christian community together before the Lord in the first place, it renews each week that bond and that presence, it expresses what happens when two people get married, when we are reconciled, when we are sick, when we die. In very simple ways, it marks the mornings, the meals and the nights of our lives.

Christian Initiation of Adults

Every society that wishes to continue must admit new members. This is true of the bowling league, the university, the Teamsters, the United States, and the churches. In some societies, very little may be involved in the process of gaining admittance: when you wish to become a member of a book-of-the-month club, you just send in the coupon and the check. At another extreme, the television drama *Roots* depicted the rites by which young men gained admission to adulthood in an African tribe. The seriousness which surrounds the admission of new members, the length of time involved, the amount of back-and-forth between the one asking admission and the group itself—these would seem to be some of the signs by which we evaluate how vital and important the group is to its members.

Moreover, the customs that make up the initiation will usually tell the candidate much about the group and the group much about the candidate. It is not unlike the time of engagement before marriage: if these two are to spend much of their lives together, it is worth the trouble of the initiation time. The rites which are developed and used over and over again during the time of initiation of new members are those which experience has shown to work: they let candidate and church make good decisions about one another.

The Catholic church has been slowly rediscovering its rites for the Christian initiation of adults. The patterns in these rites are based on those developed in the early centuries of the church when many adults came and sought admission to the Christian communities. Dioceses and national assemblies of bishops are moving very slowly because so much is at stake: it takes awhile to move from the recent tradition of convert classes and private instruction before baptism to the process of initiation envisioned in the new rites.

The new rite presumes a period of initiation lasting at least a year, and perhaps several years. In the first stage, the person hears the preaching of the gospel. This is a time of inquiry, not to be rushed. A second stage is called the catechumenate. It begins when the candidate formally enters the "order of the catechumens" which, like the "order of the baptized," is a way of belonging in the church. During this time, which may last several years, formation happens through contact with the church community and especially with catechists; catechumens may be present for the liturgy of the word, and the community's keeping of the Christian year is to be the great teacher of its way of living and of believing. When both community and catechumen judge that the time is right, the rite of "election" takes place, meaning that the catechumens are now "the elect," the chosen. This happens at the start of Lent. Lent is to be a period of purification and is marked by special rites of "scrutiny" at the Sunday Masses. The church prays that the candidates will be free of all evil. Then, after the fast of Good Friday and Holy Saturday, the elect profess their faith at the Easter Vigil, are baptized and confirmed and share for the first time in the eucharist. During the fifty days of Eastertime the newly baptized continue to come together. This is to be a time for showing them the fullness of the church's life.

Liturgy is where the church puts its life together, so it is at liturgy that the church expresses itself toward the candidates—from their enrollment in the catechumenate until the end of their first Eastertime as Christians. In coming years, these rites will more and more be ways for the local church to be aware of its catechumens, to be stirred by their presence. But liturgy has to express what is real in people's lives. So these rites of initiation must gather up what is really going on: the candidates learning of Christ from those who make up the church, and the church members themselves learning Christ anew from these candidates.

Reflections

The initiation of adults presumes a great deal more than just a sacramental ritual bath. If we reduce adult initiation to the rites at the font, we rob the convert of the much needed love and support and Christian witness that only a flesh and blood community can give. The whole process of becoming a Christian, as proposed in the Rite of Christian Initiation of Adults, requires the community's involvement in the candidate's journey to baptism. The community passes on the living tradition of faith in a way that no *one* person or catechism could ever do. Behind all the rites and catechetical preparation, there must be a strong sense of welcome. The community must open its arms and warmly receive new members and so integrate them into the community.

1. Study the introduction to the Rite of Christian Initiation of Adults. How does it compare with present parish practice of receiving adults into the church?
2. Seek out some converts. What do they have to say about their initiation that could help future parish plans?
3. How can the parish minister to adults after baptism?

Infant Baptism

A baby makes a difference. Parents know that, and older brothers and sisters know it very well. Things change. They have to. Adjustments are made, and the long process begins of taking this person from total helplessness to something like maturity. Society, in the person of the neighbors and relations, medical personnel and even the business world, prepares the parents for their new lives before the birth of the baby. Showers for the mother help gather necessary equipment as well as advice. Questions about sex, weight and name get everyone through the first days. The larger society also takes notice: making future room in schools, the work place, the shopping center.

The church also marks the birth of a baby into its community. The baptism of infants is the most visible manifestation of this notice. This rite, revised after Vatican II so that it expresses the reality that this is an infant and not just a tiny adult being baptized, is a gathering of the church around the couple and their child. As with adults, initiation is initiation into a community, but here it is for the community to pledge itself to be a source of nourishment, of faith, of a gospel-filled way of life.

Parishes often ask parents to attend preparation sessions before the child is born. These are opportunities for the parents to meet the staff and the parishioners who have taken on this special ministry. Here they can discuss the commitment they make in having a child baptized, and find out something about how this parish can give them support in this commitment. After some process like this, the parents can make a decision about the baptism and the pastor can see that they are serious in their intention to have a home where the child can learn trust and love from the very first. Then the baptism is planned.

In the child's baptism, parents and community express commitment. That is why the community should be present: its support is real, not abstract. In practice, that commitment might be shown in some special minister who would work with the families before, at, and after the baptism. These ministers would be people who have gifts for getting to know people quickly and putting them at ease. They should want to show to the parents a church that is concerned to help with their real needs and is not just out to impose its own patterns on them. It is these ministers who see to it that the church does not forget the child during the years between baptism and first communion. They know how important these first years are to all that comes after, and how much parents need support at this time.

The rite of infant baptism itself should be scheduled so that it can be a festive welcoming of the child and a strong affirmation of the faith and commitment of parents and community.

The celebration may take place at Sunday Mass since the presence of the community is so important, but such Sunday baptisms should not be scheduled too often. Appropriate days would include Easter above all others, the Baptism of the Lord and perhaps the patronal feast of the parish. Within the rite, the acclamations of the assembly—voicing their support for the parents and rejoicing at the baptism itself—need to be strong: with song or applause or other clear signs. Recent documents support the preference for baptism by immersion so that the great symbol of the water, spoken of so well in its blessing, may be felt strongly by everyone present. The baptismal garment and the candle are also to be beautiful objects witnessing what has happened.

Reflections

When a young child is baptized, our attention very naturally is on the infant. But the parents deserve attention too, for they are the ones who, at this baptism of their child, commit themselves to raising their offspring in faith. They will need support and encouragement, prayer and good example to fulfill their vocation as Christian parents. These parents may be newcomers to the neighborhood or infrequent worshipers. Even for active and practicing parents the baptism of a child can be the occasion for further initiation into the church's life.

1. How can the parish family show its support to parents at the time of baptism?

2. What happens to a child between the baptism and the first year of school? What things are learned, and what directions are set? At baptism, parents promise a Christian home and the community promises to support the parents in this. How could the community show this support during the first five years of the child's life?

Confirmation

The discussion within the church about this sacrament is reflected in the variety of ages suggested for its celebration. In some places, the church confirms infants when they are baptized. In other areas, confirmation may come at first communion time. The practice in much of this country has been to confirm during the junior high years, but a few places have moved in the direction of a much later time, letting confirmation mark a more mature decision for membership in the church. There is general agreement that confirmation is historically a sacrament of initiation, along with baptism and eucharist, but disagreement as to its use in the church today.

In most places, for now, there will be celebrations of this sacrament for large groups of young people. It is important that the liturgy be a strong expression of the church's living in the Spirit, of the church's prayer that the Spirit be strong in those confirmed. Exclusive emphasis on maturity in an updated "soldiers of Christ" theology is inadequate.

In the liturgy itself, the presence of the candidates is primary. In fact, their presence should be felt by the whole parish in the weeks prior to the confirmation: by praying for them publicly, by their presence in a group (with sponsors) at Sunday Masses. At the confirmation liturgy, their individual names need to be heard, and each face seen. They are not a "confirmation class," anonymous seventh or eighth graders: they are so many persons, each of whom has requested confirmation and has been found ready, each of whom has a sponsor and the pastor to testify to that readiness. The candidates and sponsors should help in the preparation of the confirmation liturgy, learning about and experiencing especially the power and the history of the laying on of hands and the anointing with perfumed oil.

Confirmation ordinarily means the presence of the bishop. Plans for the liturgy should allow him, as presider, to relate very directly to the candidates and to the whole assembly. If the liturgy is concelebrated, it should not obscure this relationship. Within the liturgy, the bishop might be welcomed and introduced. Since he will be unfamiliar with the local practices in the liturgy, all the other ministers should be very well rehearsed in their roles and have a feeling for the overall flow of the liturgy. This can free the bishop simply to preside, to be completely present to the candidates and to the assembly.

The liturgy should move simply, without adding elements which are intended to give solemnity but, in fact, obscure or weaken the central symbols of laying on of hands, anointing and eucharist. The preparation rites set the festive mood. The liturgy of the word happens much as on any Sunday.

In the rite of confirmation, coming after the gospel, the candidates are called forward, by name, and are then addressed in the homily by the bishop. The rites that follow should make themselves felt without extended commentary or explanations. Everything should be arranged so that the imposition of hands, with the silence which comes before, can be a most powerful experience. That can happen when all attention is on the bishop and the candidates, when the silence is total, when the gesture is full and the prayer well spoken or sung, when the "Amen" is like the great Amen at the conclusion of the eucharistic prayer. Then all should be able to see the chrism, oil mixed with fragrant perfume and blessed by the bishop on Holy Thursday. The anointing rite itself is to make generous use of the oil, and it is not to be wiped off afterwards; if anything, it should be rubbed in. The fragrance should fill the whole room. The kind of container used for the oil, the use of a rich fragrance, even carrying the oil in the entrance procession and honoring it with incense: all help to turn this from a mysterious bit of tradition to a beautiful rite of the church honoring and strengthening the presence of the Holy Spirit in its members.

After the anointing, the table is prepared for the eucharist which should be a festive banquet.

Reflections

In actions more than in words the community tells the candidates for confirmation that they are welcome and needed in the church. Confirmation is a time when the whole community rejoices in the presence of the Holy Spirit, not only as a gift given to those confirmed but as a gift that fills the entire assembly with wisdom and understanding, right judgment and courage, knowledge and love and reverence.

1. How can confirmation become more of a parishwide celebration?
2. How can we avoid making confirmation look like a class exercise?

Weddings

When two people marry, the whole complex gathering of rites—some from the state, some from the family, some from the church—serves many purposes. For one, they show what all these groups think about marriage, and they try to impress these understandings on the couple. For another, they let everyone adjust to the idea that there is a new thing among us: we cannot think of these two tomorrow as we thought of them yesterday. And yet another task of the rites: some of them are meant to allow us to express sheer delight in the festival. When ritual is doing its work, all these things are happening. But there are often difficulties when it comes to the church's part in the wedding. When there is no feeling of belonging, the couple is likely to be indifferent and see what happens in the church building as only another obligation. Apart from the "style show" entrance procession of the bridal party and a favorite song or two, it may be "anything Father wants is fine with us."

The goal is a church where people feel they belong and know that the church's ritual is their own expression of what marriage means. At present, it is often possible to begin with a sense that here is a gathering of the church, the plain old church: friends and relations with all their faults and even lack of faith. It is these people, tears and sighs and hopes, who are the gathered church. It is their faith and their love, enkindled by the marrying couple and encouraged by the presider's leadership, that will celebrate the sacrament. It is a family, a community of friends, a church, that celebrates. This understanding will not allow the couple to approach the wedding as a predetermined formula indifferent to them, or as a stage for them to celebrate themselves.

Something has to be done between the church gathered here and the couple, something beyond the legal and social, something bound up with just being the church. When we find or lose a job, when we move from one place to another, when a child grows up and moves away—these are crucial moments, times for prayer, but not yet times when we call the church together. But a wedding is something more: a more profound thing, more lasting. Our hope and our faith and our support need to find ways of expression in the church's ritual that are lacking in the other social and legal rites of the wedding. In the liturgy of the wedding we seek the deepest signs of what this church here, and the whole church, believes: the thanks to God for bringing this about, the trust in God's strong grace to see it through, the intercession for the couple and for all the church and world.

The ritual is to make such things felt, seen, heard and touched. With songs, processions, greetings, prayers, scriptures and silent reflection, the assembled friends and family are to be joined with the couple. In such a spirit, there can be a right moment for the couple to answer the questions put to them and to reply about their freedom, about fidelity, about a Christian home and family. And there can be a moment for the vows, a very strong moment, with firm words spoken to the partner so that all can hear and can respond with some sign of affirmation. The ring expresses in one of our most ancient symbols the union and the hopes that it lasts forever. The blessing of the marriage, which comes sometime later if the eucharist is celebrated, should be for all present a chance to voice all that is in their hearts for the future good of these two.

There is more than choosing among the alternatives for scripture selections or picking out good songs. There is the presumption that the rite itself is strong: a presider and other ministers who do their tasks well, a flow to the ritual that creates some community among the guests and lets them express what is in their hearts, a place for the couple to make these vows before the Lord and the church.

Reflections

Much of the discussion about a wedding liturgy can begin and end with the selection of music, and perhaps of scriptures. That's important, but there is much more to be considered. There is the gathering time and the procession, role of bride and groom (ministers of the sacrament), role of the assembly and the inclusion of particular ethnic rituals.

The assembly's role is most often ignored. Usually it appears they have gathered to watch the action or photograph it rather than participate in it. And yet the celebration of Christian marriage is really a community celebration. The whole church is blessed in this couple. There is a great joy in the witnessing the community does.

As the assembly is brought into the celebration, their participation will be a real support to the marrying couple to live out their commitment.

1. Why do you think so many engaged couples will settle for "anything Father wants"?
2. How could a congregation better express its joy and gratitude at the wedding liturgy?
3. What resources are available in your parish to help couples prepare the wedding liturgy?

Reconciliation

In the family, the school, the place of work, in any community there must be attention to healing. People are going to hurt each other, are going to let the hurt done to them grow into a greater hurt done to someone else. Choices are going to be made based on something other than the greatest good of all. Whatever way such things show themselves, we know in small and great ways the presence of evil—not just out there but inside. And we try, when we can, to find the ways to bring healing.

The church, every church, every gathering that professes to live by the words of the scriptures and to find itself in the breaking of bread, knows that all the hurting and all the healing goes to the heart of what being church is about: that God is greater than evil, that God has loved us despite the evil that we do, that there is reconciliation. Every gathering of the church proclaims this. Such direction toward reconciliation, not just as an insight of theology but as a reality in our communities, is especially celebrated in the eucharist. In the one loaf and one cup, in the praying of the Our Father, in the greeting of peace, and in the common eating and drinking of the Lord's body and blood we share a vision of God's kingdom when all the hurt we do each other ends. But the church is never satisfied with a "pie in the sky when we die" vision: the eating and the drinking in holy communion are lies if they do not reflect a present striving.

The church knows rites other than eucharist which focus on the reconciliation of an individual with the larger community, or which mark our common effort to repent, to struggle against evil. The season of Lent developed not only around the initiation of new Christians, but also to mark the acts of penance and reconciliation by those who had seriously offended the Lord's commandments and the ways of the community. Lent became a time when the whole church sought mightily to turn from ways of evil and walk in the way of the Lord.

While we are discovering the dimensions of reconciliation present in the eucharist and are seeking what the season of Lent can be for us today, we also renew the rites of reconciliation themselves. One direction here, which seems to reflect the way we are experiencing evil and the greater grace of God, is toward communal penance services. Perhaps these are associated with Lent or with other recurring days (as the ember days were) so that patterns are established. The rites themselves, with the reading of scripture and much silence, appropriate music and some gesture of reconciliation, must be planned and done well so that they bear the weight of what is being expressed. People are more and more aware that sin is not something that can be isolated in small, individual portions. Prejudice, hunger, war-making, these have made it so clear that evil is contagious and large in our world and touches all of us. And we have become more accustomed to seeing how our lives move in large directions, how the ways we share in evil or in good cannot readily be isolated: things connect, grow. We strive to let grace more and more be our way.

All of that we want to express in ritual. Sometimes it is best done in the large gathering of the church, and sometimes in the simple meeting of individual and confessor. In the latter case, we need to be exploring the possibilities of the new rite which stresses prayer, scripture reading and the laying on of hands, as well as the dialogue between individual and confessor.

Reflections

Reconciliation, like all church rituals, is more than a ritual: it is the way of life the church has. The healing nature of the church is to be evident in all the parish does. Every sinner must know that he/she is welcome in the community where mercy and compassion await. And the community cannot wait until the alienated seek reconciliation, they must get the word out fast and firmly that forgiveness and healing are gifts freely given. For any of us to pretend that we have no wounds, or that they will heal themselves, is an illusion. We need God's healing forgiveness and we need each other to be assured that the forgiveness is real.

1. How can a life of reconciliation be fostered in a parish?
2. Do you know the eucharistic prayers for reconciliation? Are they ever appropriately used in the parish?

Anointing of the Sick

Even groups of people who have organized to educate, to play ball, or just to make money are likely to take notice when one in the group is hurt or sick. We have ways of responding: sending cards, sending flowers, telephoning, going to visit. The words we use in such situations take on some familiar patterns as we offer good wishes, reassurances, jokes. We seem to know there is healing in our presence, in person or in a gift, and in familiar words.

As the church, we have from the prophets and from Jesus no doubt about the importance of visiting and caring for the sick. In an organized way, this has been one of the great works of the church: the hospitals founded and staffed by religious sisters. In its best moments, concern for the sick and for all who cannot defend themselves causes the church to raise its voice against any kind of oppression.

From the first, continuing the way Jesus cared for the sick, the church has gathered to pray for those who are suffering. To show this concern, to allow the assembled church (whether few or many) to put the sick person before the Lord, there is the laying on of hands. This brings a sense of solidarity: to the one who is sick and to those who are healthy. It is perhaps our richest symbol, this simple touching in silence. To those who are sick, the laying on of hands shows what is really true: they are never alone, never cut off from the community. But the gesture must be true, must not be alone, must not be cut off from the community. The church must be telling the truth when it lays on hands. This is not "administering a sacrament," but rather letting the sacrament embody what is happening between the community and one who is sick. The title of the new rite of anointing makes this clear: *Pastoral Care of the Sick.*

The anointing itself is not to be the only time of prayer with those who are sick. The parish should be helping those who have a special ministry to the sick learn how to be with and pray with the sick. The new rite makes this clear simply by the fact that it is found within a collection of rites called *Pastoral Care of the Sick: Rites of Anointing and Viaticum.* Here we see that the anointing is but one time of prayer with those who are sick. The parish's ministers of care also visit the sick, pray with them, bring them holy communion. Clergy, deacons and all ministers of care need a firm grasp of the approach and the particulars of these revised rites for the sick and dying which were published in 1983.

The people of a church should be aware that this sacrament, and other times of prayer which should surround it, can be celebrated when there is serious illness of any kind, and that the very young as well as the elderly may need the prayer of the church. Learning about the sacrament may well happen through the good practice of communal celebrations, where many sick and elderly persons gather with other members of the church. In a nursing home or in the parish church, the community gathers to pray with and for the sick and elderly. Such occasions need careful planning (not only of the liturgy but of transportation and other details), but can become a regular expression of the life of this church.

Reflections

Consider the power of touch. What has it meant to you in illness, or when you helped to heal with your power of touch?

One of the ways the community can express its concerns for members who are ill is to plan a communal celebration of the sacrament of anointing of the sick, and to do this within the celebration of the eucharist. Here, in the community setting, the anointed can experience in a strong way the loving care of the Christian family. But this involves more than just the scheduling. Well before the liturgy there has to be personal contact with those who will be anointed. And arrangements must be made for transportation. It is a good occasion to call people to service in the ministry of healing.

1. How might a communal celebration of the anointing of the sick affect the community's understanding of the sacrament?
2. Is there an appropriate day or time of year that would be well suited for an annual liturgy of the anointing of the sick?

Funerals

As at birth and marriage, so at death the rites of a community must serve several purposes. They will convey much of how death is understood in the group, and of what relationship there might be between the living and dead. They may also be able to contain something of the meaning of this individual's life. And the rites will handle the time of transition: from life with this person present in the community, to life with this person absent. This recognizes that death ordinarily brings a group—the family, neighborhood, church—into a different way of being. Changes like that are always difficult. They may challenge the existence of the group itself, and at the least call for people to take on new roles and new understandings.

Rites, however, are not and cannot be rational attempts to do all these things. They are the ways people do these things for themselves, and they work at levels far deeper than the rational.

The rites that surround death manifest very clearly a problem in our culture. The common practices of the mortuaries and cemeteries have their messages about the meaning of death, about this individual, about how grief is handled. Seldom do these have any relation to the convictions expressed in the rituals of the church. As with weddings, the church ritual is often the loser: it is treated as one of the things that Father does, or as support for the message of the funeral director. Parishes concerned with the ways that the church's ritual can be a strong and worthy expression of our faith will set about the task of studying the rites and options available, of forming a ministry of those who can help grieving families to make the rites their own, of seeking to educate funeral and cemetery directors to the church's best practice, and of using the month of November each year to ponder death and the communion of saints.

In particular, the parish will be concerned to minister to the dying and to mourners. The church's prayer with the dying is not "extreme unction" (now understood and practiced as the anointing of the sick), but viaticum, final communion. There are also many beautiful prayers in our tradition which praise God for the love that God has shown to this person in life, and express deep confidence in the communion of saints, the community which transcends death. These prayers continue through the moment of death and may end with the blessing of the body. In some cases, it may be that a priest or a deacon will be present, but more and more we should know these as the prayers of family and friends.

The wake service is a combining of structured and unstructured moments. The ritual involved should be in continuity with the less formal moments of gathering and greeting, sharing stories and memories, offering sympathy. The wake will often be more intimate than the funeral, and it centers far more on the one who had died. It can be a strong beginning for the long process of coming to terms with life now that this person is gone. The community is able to show its support in the wake, support that is to be there in weeks and months to come.

The funeral liturgy, usually with the celebration of the eucharist, allows for scripture readings and music and various other elements to be chosen by the family or others. In this liturgy and in the rites that take place by the side of the grave, the church holds parting and communion in tension: there is the final commendation of the deceased to the Lord, and the realism of the grave itself, while we console ourselves in faith in our communion with the saints and our waiting for the resurrection of the dead and the life of the world to come. The rites take these things and give them powerful expression in song, word and gesture.

Reflections

The family of one who has died, and all friends that make up a community, want a "good" funeral. But what makes such a funeral? Have you participated in some? What would make your own funeral good?

Our rites are not attempts to hide grief and sorrow. The sense of loss and emptiness are not denied by the Christian liturgy. At the wake, family and friends must be helped to face death. They should be given the opportunity to share aloud the memories of the one who had died. The story of the dead Christian must be told: family and friends must not leave all the words to the clergy who may not have known the deceased very well. The *Rite of Christian Burial* suggests that at the final commendation in the church the family may wish to speak to those assembled. This does not mean the funeral becomes one long eulogy, but that there is place for personal expression.

Family and friends are not to be coldly subjected to the funeral ritual, but brought into the rites and prayers, making the liturgy of the church a real aid to the bereaved in burying their dead.

1. How might the family be helped to participate more in the funeral rites at the wake? At the church? At the cemetery?
2. Apart from the funeral rites, how can a parish foster a good spirituality of death?

The Liturgy of the Hours

Not too many people would even be able to identify this title. Why then does it belong in these notes about the familiar prayers of Catholics? A long time ago we lost much of the poetic richness that praying at the morning and evening had for our ancestors when hymns and psalms, known by heart, gave the individual and the household ways to praise and thank God constantly. In more recent times, substitutes were found: the prayers called "morning offering," or the act of contrition, as well as the angelus and other prayers related to the time of day. For some, these have failed and there is apparently nothing in their place.

Something similar has happened with our use of rituals apart from the Mass. Many popular devotions (Sacred Heart, Sorrowful Mother, etc.) developed during the centuries when the liturgy of the Mass was not something in which Catholics could fully participate. These devotions were usually in the language of the people, used popular hymns, and often involved a very great use of movement, gesture, and objects such as incense and images. Participation in such devotions has dwindled.

There is a vacuum, and it is a problem. It is in these non-eucharistic prayers and devotions that Catholics have learned to pray: as individuals, in the family and in small communities. Without such habits to provide the day-in, day-out prayers, to train us in how to pray, to keep prayer present, we have no way to prepare to pray the eucharist, no way to learn how to use prayers in the large gathering of the church, no way to let the eucharist echo through our week. We learn to pray by praying, and we learn to pray the Mass through the many ways that ritual prayer can enter our lives throughout the day and week. Discovering the forms and rhythms of prayer which will come honestly to people today must have a high priority.

To suggest that the liturgy of the hours may do this need not bring visions of trying to popularize the bulky breviary usually associated with the clergy. That brieviary is, in fact, the product of a history that began with the simple prayer of all Christians. In the monasteries this became a very complex pattern of prayers and was lost to the people. Today some are searching for the roots of this liturgy of the hours, what was best in its earliest forms, in hope that a truly "popular" form of morning and evening prayer may enter again into the daily or weekly prayer of parishes and individuals.

In its simplest form, the praising and thanking of God each morning and evening are not something to be written down. It is a prayer for memory, known by heart. The basic prayers for this are the Lord's

Prayer, intercessions and psalms. They can take the repetition, can bear the weight of being used every day in a way that most texts simply cannot. For the individual, the prayer of morning or evening might be one or two short psalms, perhaps with some shorter acclamations and time for reflection. When several pray together, in the parish setting or at home, simple hymns would be added and prayers of intercession. On Sunday afternoons and on some weekday mornings or evenings during Lent, or on festival days, a parish could begin to develop a slightly more elaborate liturgy of the hours. In any of these settings, the reading of the scriptures might have a place.

The daily living of the faith needs to be strengthened with simple prayer, rites of prayer in that they are regular and somewhat fixed. These are to be in the heart when rising and preparing for the day, and when coming to table together, and when retiring at night. In a more elaborate way, they are to be the gathered church's prayer between one Sunday eucharist and the next. They do not need to be created from nothing: we have them, have always had them, as Jesus himself knew them so well, in the psalms and the reading of our scripture.

Reflections

How do the Angelus, morning prayers, the sign of the cross at night fulfill the work of this kind of prayer?

In the liturgy of the hours the church—and we are the church—sanctifies the day. This presumes a sensitivity to the rhythm of the day. We need to see the rising of the sun and its setting as a sign of God caring for creation. The hope is that the liturgy of the hours could become a satisfying human ritual celebrating the movement of night and day in our lives.

The *General Instruction on the Liturgy of the Hours* provides a basic understanding of the church's theology of prayer. It should be studied carefully as an introduction to the spirituality of daily prayer.

1. Other than the Mass, what forms of prayer are offered to your community?

2. What might be some occasions in your parish when the liturgy of the hours would be more appropriate than the Mass?

Resources for *Other Rites*

Fitzgerald, Timothy. *Confirmation: A Parish Celebration*. Chicago: Liturgy Training Publications, 1983.

Detailed examination of the rite of confirmation for planners and ministers.

Gusmer, Charles. *And You Visited Me: Pastoral Care of the Sick*. New York: Pueblo Publishing Company, 1984.

Development of the rites of the sick and a guide to their pastoral implementation in the parish.

Hellwig, Monika, ed. *Message of the Sacraments*. Wilmington: Michael Glazier, Inc.

Eight volumes on the sacraments by outstanding scholars/writers.

Huck, Gabe. *A Book of Family Prayer*. New York: Seabury, 1979.

Daily, seasonal and occasional prayer for the individual or household.

Huck, Gabe. *Infant Baptism in the Parish: Understanding the Rite*. Chicago: Liturgy Training Publications, 1980.

For parish planners and ministers approaching the policies and ritual for infant baptism.

Huck, Gabe. *Teach Me to Pray:* New York: Sadlier, 1982.

Basic Catholic prayers from scripture and tradition with brief notes. Arranged by time of day and season of the church's year.

Kavanagh, Aidan. *The Shape of Baptism: The Rite of Christian Initiation*. New York: Pueblo Publishing Company, 1978.

Outstanding study of the church's initiatory practices and implications of the Rite of Christian Initiation of Adults.

Lewinski, Ronald. *Welcoming the New Catholic*. Chicago: Liturgy Training Publications, 1983 (revised edition).

The introduction and use of the Rite of Christian Initiation of Adults *in the parish.*

Martos, Joseph. *Doors to the Sacred*. New York: Doubleday, 1981.

History of the rites through the present.

Mayer, Laurence, and Scheible, Alan. *Evening Prayer in the Parish*. Chicago: Liturgy Training Publications, 1981.

Background and leaders' books for a simple parish celebration of vespers.

The Rites. New York: Pueblo Publishing Company, 1984 (second edition).

Complete introductions and rites for adult initiation, infant baptism, confirmation, penance, marriage, pastoral care of the sick (new rite), and funerals.

Rutherford, Richard. *The Death of a Christian: The Rite of Funerals.* New York: Pueblo Publishing Company, 1980.

The history, theology and celebration of the reformed rites for the burial of the dead.

Schmemann, Alexander. *Of Water and the Spirit.* Crestwood NY: St. Vladimir's Seminary Press, 1974.

A study of initiation in the Orthodox tradition which offers many insights for those of other rites.

Seaman, Marie. *Baptism Is a Beginning.* Chicago: Liturgy Training Publications, 1980.

A series of pamphlets for parents covering the time before the baptism and until the child is four years old.

Searle, Mark. *Christening: The Making of Christians.* Collegeville: The Liturgical Press, 1982.

History and detailed study of the ritual for infant baptism and confirmation.

Simons, Thomas. *Blessings for God's People.* Notre Dame: Ave Maria Press, 1983.

Daily, annual and occasional blessings gathered from many sources.

In Conclusion

The *Directory for Masses with Children* is a 1973 document from the Vatican's Sacred Congregation for Divine Worship. What it has to say goes beyond planning Masses with children and is important for any consideration of how the church prays.

In the introductory paragraphs, the document provides some fine statements about the creation of a whole environment, a way of living, in which prayer will be possible and real for children—or for any of us. "Children are prepared for eucharistic communion and introduced more deeply into its meaning. It is not right to separate such liturgical and eucharistic formation from the general human and Christian education of children. Indeed it would be harmful if liturgical formation lacked such a foundation." (8) The preparation for praying the eucharist is not learning about eucharistic liturgy, it is simply learning to pray, to be at home with song and gesture and all that our rituals involve. But this is not something which can exist in a different world, its own box. For example: the holiness of the altar table and of the sharing in the bread and cup is not to be learned in isolation. A sense for that holiness depends on the child (anyone) experiencing in the family a sense for the holiness of all food and of the meal taken together. When these experiences are deep and rich, a person can have a feeling for what we are about at eucharist. Without that, the liturgy necessarily becomes something apart from what I am and do.

This puts our prayer in a larger and realistic context. Teaching children to pray, for example, is not first a matter of learning the Lord's Prayer, or having the family together each Sunday at Mass. It is a matter of a way of living: what things are important to the family, how prayer centers them. Song together at table, thanksgiving and intercession at bedtime, time for reading and reflection on the Sunday scriptures, customs and prayers to mark the seasons—these are learning to pray when they are important to the parents, part of normal life. Day by day and week by week they reflect the sense for God's presence that fills all of life.

When people gather for eucharist, the *Directory* tells us, there are some qualities which should be observed: "In this way even if children already have some feeling for God and the things of God, they may also experience the human values which are found in the eucharistic celebration, depending upon their age and personal progress. These values are the activity of the community, exchange of greetings, capacity to listen and to seek and grant pardon, expression of gratitude, experience of symbolic actions, a meal of friendship, and festive celebration." (9) That rather awesome list is describing the *human experience*. We may or may not be able to verbalize it, but after a parish Sunday Mass, we should have a sense for having been at a meal of friendship, a festive celebration. We should feel like we have really put words and gestures on our thanksgiving to God. The *Directory* wants us to be careful of saying what happens at Mass in theological language, or on some spiritual level, if we have not tended first to the level of human experience on which all else depends.

And that has been a unifying element through these pages: to discover how much we know and feel about good ritual, yet often do not bring to our liturgy work because we have not made the connections, or have thought the church's prayer to be only a matter of history and documents and rubrics. It is much more a matter of real people and their very real spirit.

Resources

Ritual Books

These basic texts should be part of the sacristy library of every Roman Catholic parish. They are available from various publishers.

Lectionary for Mass (1970).

Sacramentary (1985).

Book of Blessings (1989).

Catholic Household Blessings and Prayers (1988).

Holy Communion and Worship of the Eucharist outside Mass (1974).

Liturgical Calendar.

Liturgy of the Hours (1970, 1973, 1975).

Order of Christian Funerals (1989).

Pastoral Care of the Sick (1983).

Rite of Baptism for Children (1970).

Rite of Christian Initiation of Adults (1988).

Rite of Marriage (1970).

Rite of Penance (1976).

Liturgical Documents

Code of Canon Law (1983).

Documents on the Liturgy, 1963–1979: Conciliar, Papal and Curial Texts (Collegeville: The Liturgical Press, 1982).

The Liturgy Documents (Chicago: Liturgy Training Publications, 1985).

Periodicals

Assembly (Center for Pastoral Liturgy, PO Box 81, Notre Dame IN 46556), five times a year.

Bishops' Committee on the Liturgy Newsletter (United States Catholic Conference, 3211 Fourth Street NE, Washington DC 20017-1194), ten times a year.

Catechumenate: A Journal of Christian Initiation (Liturgy Training Publications [LTP], 1800 North Hermitage Avenue, Chicago IL 60622-1101), six times a year.

Environment and Art Letter: A Forum on Architecture and the Arts for the Parish (LTP), monthly.

Liturgy: Journal of the Liturgical Conference (The Liturgical Conference, 1017 12th Street NW, Washington DC 20005), quarterly.

Liturgy 90 (LTP), eight times a year.

National Bulletin on Liturgy (Publications Service, Canadian Conference of Catholic Bishops, 90 Parent Avenue, Ottawa, Ontario K1N 7B1, Canada), four times a year.

Pastoral Music (National Association of Pastoral Musicians, 225 Sheridan Street NW, Washington DC 20011), six times a year.

Worship (The Order of St. Benedict, St. John's Abbey, Collegeville MN 56321), six times a year.